ONLY A
THOUGHT
AWAY

ABOUT THE AUTHOR

© Kathleen Mathews

Bestselling author Patrick Mathews has helped countless people around the world with his gift of communicating with those who have crossed over to the Other Side. His acute, heightened level of connection with spirit, along with his personality and heartfelt compassion, make him one of the most nationally known and sought-after mediums today.

From parents, teachers, and celebrities to psychologists, athletes, and law enforcement agencies, individuals call upon Patrick from every walk of life. He is committed to helping people transform the quality of their lives by confirming not only the existence of their loved ones in spirit, but the continuing relationship they have with them as well!

Patrick and his sister, author Kathy Mathews, enjoy giving lectures, workshops, and demonstrations of his gift throughout the country. These events have a profound impact for those who attend them.

Patrick has appeared on numerous television shows airing on ABC, CBS, NBC, PBS, and cable networks, as well as many top radio shows around the country, including the *Ryan Seacrest Show*. Patrick was also a featured medium on the Travel Channel's hit television shows *Most Haunted* and *Most Haunted Live*, which was seen worldwide. His bestselling books have helped countless people around the world to understand and to recognize their own continuing connections with loved ones in spirit. They have been published in numerous languages in various countries.

PATRICK MATHEWS

ONLY A THOUGHT AWAY

Keeping in Touch With Your Loved Ones in Spirit

Llewellyn Publications
Woodbury, Minnesota

First Edition
First Printing, 2019

Book format by Samantha Penn
Cover design by Kevin R. Brown
Cover photo by Kathy Mathews
Editing by Annie Burdick
Part page art by Llewellyn Art Department

Llewellyn is a registered trademark of Llewellyn Worldwide Ltd.

Library of Congress Cataloging-in-Publication Data (Pending)

ISBN: 978-0-7387-5699-8

Llewellyn Worldwide Ltd. does not participate in, endorse, or have any authority or responsibility concerning private business transactions between our authors and the public.
    All mail addressed to the author is forwarded, but the publisher cannot, unless specifically instructed by the author, give out an address or phone number.
    Any internet references contained in this work are current at publication time, but the publisher cannot guarantee that a specific location will continue to be maintained. Please refer to the publisher's website for links to authors' websites and other sources.

Llewellyn Publications
A Division of Llewellyn Worldwide Ltd.
2143 Woodbury Drive
Woodbury, MN 55125-2989, U.S.A.
www.llewellyn.com

Printed in the United States of America

OTHER BOOKS BY PATRICK MATHEWS

Never Say Goodbye
Forever With You
Everlasting Love

DEDICATION

I dedicate this book to all who are searching for understanding of the infinite possibilities and continuous connections to those in spirit that they love.

The love you share is *the* link between this world and the next that makes the continuing connection *you* have with them possible.

CONTENTS

Acknowledgments

I want to first give a great big shout out to my sister Kathy Mathews. We had no idea where this journey was going to take us when we first started on this path, and we continue to discover and learn something new every day. Thank you for all that you do for others, but most of all, what you do for me…

Much love to my wonderful parents, James and Florence Mathews. Your love and spiritual guidance place a smile on my face every day.

Thanks again to my literary agent, Al Zuckerman. To someone who brought the *Twilight* series to the world, and who also thought my books could bring another type of "light" into this world, your kindness and praise is never forgotten.

To all the wonderful people at Llewellyn Publications, thank you for your ever-continuous support with bringing my books to the world.

I am being TOLD by my eleven-year-old niece, Riley Sublette, that her name has to be in my book ... *See, I told you I would!*

To the many media outlets who have been gracious enough to have Kathy and me on, thank you for helping us to get our message out there and for putting up with our sometimes crazy antics! Also, a special shout out to Melissa Chase (The Best!) and Jack Lauterback (OTH 4ever!)

Thank you to Dr. Glenn Weiner for helping to connect a little science to my "gift."

Kathleen Marusak, you add joy to the process.

I also want to mention all who help both Kathy and me at our live events. You help to bring the other definition of "Spirit" to life! Especially you, John Burns ... (Don't let this go to your head)

To all my friends who put up with all the "ghosts" that are around from time to time, I told you they don't bite ... most of the time, anyway!

And last but certainly not least, a very special "Thank You" to everyone whose stories are part of this book. The experiences you share help to teach others far and wide that connections with loved ones in spirit continue always.

INTRODUCTION

In writing this book, I wanted you the reader to understand that even though Heaven is a place that our souls transition to when this physical body dies, it is not some far-off, distant place. You see, Heaven, the Other Side, or however you refer to it, is actually all around us, only separated by a different set of physics. And therefore, as close as Heaven really is, so too are those you love in spirit.

Being a medium, I have the ability to make a connection with those in spirit and to receive messages from them. And how am I able to do this? Well that's a good question and one that I too have wondered. As a child, I would see spirits every now and then. They would come to me usually when I least expected, and these "visits" would be relatively short. And so, growing up, I was Patrick, the kid who could see ghosts.

As an adult, as I went on with my life, my "gift" started to come more toward the forefront. It was a "knowing" I felt inside that I had to discover what this gift I had was. Just as with any gift a person may possess, such as singing, dancing, and art, I had to learn how to build upon it and to control the gift of connecting with spirits. So, through trial and error, meditating and studying, I came to the point that I could control and use my gift of communicating with those in spirit at will.

It was then I decided to become a medium, as I saw that this gift I had could change people's lives for the better. And over the course of many years as a medium, I have spoken with countless people, and even more in spirit, helping to confirm not only the continuing existence of those in spirit, but also the continuing connection they have with those they love here.

But is having this ability of communication with spirit something that is connected physically to me, or is it spiritual, meaning it's a connection with my soul?

As you will read in this book, I found the possible answer to the question of why I am able to connect with those in spirit. But make no mistake, you make connections with your loved ones in spirit as well!

Every day, your loved ones in spirit are with you, helping you and guiding you, in the miraculous ways that spirits are able to. But most of the time, these connections between you and those in spirit go unnoticed. And the great news is that by learning and understanding how connections with your loved ones in spirit take place, along with the subtle (and sometimes not-so-subtle) signs they are giving you, it will become more apparent that just like me, you too are in touch with Heaven.

In Part 1, The Presence of Heaven, I explain how although it seems as if Heaven and those in spirit are far away, in fact they are not, and they are actually a lot closer than you think! You see, Heaven and your loved ones in spirit are not actually separated from you by distance, but only by "physics." And although your loved ones in spirit enjoy all that Heaven is by experiencing the physics they are now a part of, they still can and do continue to be a part of our physics as well, making it possible for them to share in your life and guide you in ways only those in spirit can!

I also share my own personal experience putting science to the test through brain mapping with a top researcher in the field, in order to prove how my brain in fact does change when I am connecting with spirits! The results surprised even the expert...

Part 2, Understanding the Grieving Process, helps you to understand how the grieving process works and that you are not alone in how you experience it. Having a loved one pass into spirit may be one of the most painful experiences you will ever go through. Breaking it down and understanding the process of grief, and accepting the healing aspect of it, can help you to come out of it a stronger, better person than ever before.

Part 3, How to Keep in Touch With your Loved Ones in Spirit, explains that even though there is a different set of physics that separates you from your loved ones in spirit, you can in fact continue your relationship and your connection with them! All signs are not created equal! Those in spirit can and do give physical signs of their continuing connection with you, and understanding how they do this will help you know what to ask for and what to look for.

It is also important to understand that although signs are great, "connections" with those in spirit are even greater! Connections with loved ones in spirit take place on a daily basis, but will usually just go unnoticed, and most of the time they are pushed off as products of imagination. The more you understand how and when these connections happen (which is explained in this part) the stronger and more noticeable they will become!

Part 4, Stories of Living My Life With the Afterlife, shares some of the things I have experienced being a medium. Although most people are in contact with spirits—or should I say spirits are in contact with them—most of the time this can go unnoticed.

This is not true for me…

I am always aware of those in spirit and this can lead to some very interesting and unique experiences, which I share in this part of the book. I also answer some of the most common questions that I am asked, as well as share some of my thoughts and experiences that I know you will enjoy with My Last Words in part 5.

———

So, in reading this book, the one thing that I want you to take away and always remember is that your loved ones in spirit are truly *only a thought away…*

PART 1
THE PRESENCE OF HEAVEN

Many people believe that science cannot co-exist with God, Heaven, spirits, and the afterlife.

I totally disagree.

In my opinion, all that the afterlife is and consists of is based on physics—physics that are shared by this world we live in and others we can never even imagine.

So, could science ever prove there is a Heaven and an afterlife? It may one day, depending on how far science in this physical life develops.

Think about it: there was a time in this world when it was not understood why water would turn to steam or even where the steam ended up. And just because at that point in time, science could not explain why this transition occurred, it still did not make that steam any less real. But science did eventually conclude why this happens, thereby explaining the physics of this action taking place.

The same holds true for the afterlife; just because science cannot explain it yet does not make the afterlife any less real.

1. Heavenly Physics

It's hard to try to comprehend exactly what or where Heaven is until you understand some of the basics of physics. Now, before you start to think that you don't, I promise that you do, so bear with me and keep reading!

The simple definition for physics is that it is the science that deals with matter, energy, motion, and force. It is the explanations of the "hows and whys" things are the way they are on earth. The physical life we live in has its own rules and structure. Therefore, there is a reason an apple will fall from a tree and why clouds float in the sky. Most people cannot give an exact scientific reason why these things can take place, but they know there is a law of nature for why it does. But with any science, our understanding is limited to only the physics of this world we live in and to what has been discovered or understood so far.

Heaven not only shares our physics, but has much more ...

As science explains, it is impossible to destroy energy; it can only change form. And there is no question that our body consists of energy, as does our soul. So when our energy (our soul) leaves the body, this is what is known as passing into spirit. Our soul body now exists entirely without our physical body and transitions into the next stage of our continuing life.

The soul body is in some way a mirror image of the body a person had in this physical life. The only difference between the two is that the soul has absolutely no imperfections. For those who are handicapped, deformed, or ill in any physical or mental way, their soul is not. Once a person passes into spirit, leaving this physical body, they are once again in their truest, purest, and healthiest form. Within our soul lies a conscience and the sum of knowledge and feelings that makes us who we truly are.

Heaven itself is as an actual place, one that has its own set of physics, more than we could ever imagine or even comprehend, for that matter. It is the place to where all living energy transitions. Heaven is not off in some distant place, but actually exists in another plane, one that transcends the known physics of this world.

Here's another way to look at it: Think of yourself living in the ocean. There is a whole world that exists underwater, one with its own set of physics and laws of nature. But looking up, on top of the water lies a whole new world, a world that has air, trees, birds, people, and a sky, just to name a few things. This new physical place has always been surrounding the water, but could only be discovered once the transition from in the water to out of the water took place.

This is the same as passing into spirit: a whole new physical world opens, one that has always been around you, just not seen, a place we call Heaven. And it's not really hard to believe that something like this could actually exist and be around you.

Living your everyday life, no matter if you are inside your house or outside enjoying the world, the fact of the matter is that you are constantly surrounded by energy waves. Waves of energy are constantly beaming out from cell phone towers, television towers, and satellites in space. And within this energy is information, which is transmitting all around you, including through your devices, like phones, televisions, radios, and GPS, just to name a few. You don't feel this energy, you don't see this energy, you don't even hear this energy; that is until you turn on any of these devices and BAM ... here in front of you is physical proof that these energy signals are, in fact, all around you!

If you didn't have any of these devices, there would be no proof of this informational energy even existing, but that doesn't make it any less real. This is the same way it is with your loved ones in spirit. Just because you don't see them, feel them, or hear them around you, doesn't make them any less real.

Most people will feel a loved one's presence, but usually will push it off as wishful thinking. The more a person is open to this actually taking place, the stronger the connection can become.

Terry had it all going for herself. Moving from a small town and now living in a big city, starting an exciting new job as a fashion consultant, this all was something she had worked very hard to achieve. But with all of this, she had felt the most happiness with a new boyfriend who she fell for at first sight.

It seemed everything, for once, was going Terry's way, as if nothing could stop her happiness. That is until the day her mother called her with the bad news ... a tragic loss; her father had suddenly passed away.

It was hard for Terry to comprehend what her mother was saying to her over the phone. How could her father be dead? How could this be? He was fine when she last saw her parents. Terry just couldn't believe this was happening and she was beyond distraught at this news.

She and her father had been so close, two peas in a pod. They did everything together. He went to every event, soccer game, school play, and he even framed most of her drawings to show off her artistic skills, something that slightly embarrassed her at times, but she knew how it brought a smile to his face. They were inseparable. Even as an adult, her father always referred to her as daddy's little girl.

Terry had just begun planning to take a trip back home to see her mother and father and couldn't wait to share with them all the wonderful and exciting events taking place in her life. But as in many cases, the days turned into weeks and the weeks turned into months and time just simply slipped away from her.

It was an agonizing and grief-filled year for Terry after the passing of her father. Still distraught, Terry came to me in hopes of hearing from her father to get some kind of relief. She was very nervous and started to shake like a leaf, so I tried to calm her down a bit.

"It's so nice to meet you, Terry!" I said to her. "I can tell you may be a little nervous, but I promise you those nerves will disappear in a minute or two."

She looked at me, took a deep breath, and smiled just a bit. "Thank you, Patrick."

At that moment, I noticed a spirit starting to approach me: her father.

I said, "While we have been talking, a father just came to me. Is this who you wanted me to connect with for you?"

Terry put her head down and started to weep. "It is," she said. She looked up and asked, "How did you know that?"

"Normally," I explained, "spirits will wait until we are ready to connect with them, but this gentleman is breaking my rules a bit and can't wait."

This brought a slight smile to Terry's face.

"Like I said, he's already here and ready to talk, so give me a moment and let me connect with him and see what he has to say."

Even though I am able to sense when a spirit is standing next to me, I then have to take a moment to make a connection with them in order for the communication to begin. Now, when I say connection, this means I just open my senses up and start to listen to what they want to say. A spirit will communicate with me verbally, meaning speaking to me; visually, meaning showing me images and visuals in my mind; and by giving me different emotions and feelings. Usually a spirit will communicate in all these ways.

Terry clenched her hands, rubbing them anxiously.

"Okay, now your father is communicating to me that he had a fast passing," I said.

Terry replied with a shaky voice. "Yes, he did."

I continued, "He is giving me a feeling in my heart; I take it he had a heart attack."

Tears streamed down her face and Terry replied through her tears. "He did. One night he went to sleep and he never woke up."

"I'm so sorry to hear this, Terry. I know how hard an unexpected passing can be. But your father wants you to know that he did not feel a thing with his passing." Terry looked relieved. "He also wants you to know that he didn't know anything was wrong with his heart," I told her.

"I was going to ask that!" she said. "I had asked my mother if he had had any signs of something wrong and she said there had been nothing. We both wondered if there had been something that he kept hidden from us."

"Well he has answered that question, because he is telling me that he had no idea that he had anything wrong with his heart," I said to Terry.

Terry said, "That is such a relief. It would not have been like him to keep anything from my mother. I know this will make my mother very happy to hear."

"In fact, he's telling me that besides the major heart attack, he was fit as a fiddle! His words, not mine," I said with a smile. That made us both laugh.

"That is my daddy," she said with a smile of her own.

I told Terry to keep in mind that a spirit will always tell the truth to their loved ones. And if her father told her he did not know, he did not know.

I continued. "Your father tells me that there was a separation between you two, that you were away from him at the time of his passing and you had not seen him in a while."

Terry started to cry again. "I feel so guilty about this," she said. "I was planning to go see them, but I got so caught up with my work and relationship that time just slipped by."

"Don't you worry about that, your father is telling me to tell you. He knew how busy you were, and you were out there trying to achieve your dreams! He says 'Honey, life happens,' and he wants you to know how proud he and your mother are of you."

"I always hoped they were," she said. "It's because of them and how they raised me to never settle for anything less than my dreams."

"Well don't think it anymore. Know it," I said to her.

With that, her father then gave me an image of women's clothing.

"Terry, your father is showing me women's clothing. Now that means you're into clothing or he's into women's clothing ... which one?" I said smiling.

Terry laughed and excitedly said, "It's me! I had recently received a job in fashion and couldn't wait to tell them, but he passed before I could. It really broke my heart that my dad didn't get to know this."

"Well you now know that he does know it!" I said. "Remember your father has been with you every day since he passed into spirit and he keeps an eye on you and your mother more than you can ever know!"

"I was hoping that was true! I always felt that I could feel him with me from time to time, but never really knew if that was him or not," Terry said.

"Well now you know for a fact that it's him and that he's able not only to keep an eye out for you, but to guide you in your life, which makes him happy. Remember, he says, no matter how old you are, you are still his little girl!"

Terry started to cry, but this time with tears of happiness! She knew not only how proud her father was of her, but how much he loved and will continue loving her as well as guiding her ... just as daddies do for their little girls.

If you think about it, it really is pretty amazing how loved ones in spirit not only continue to be with you, but continue to be a part of your life. Because they are able to transcend between the two different sets of physics, they can enjoy all that Heaven is, while continuing to be a part of your life.

Sort of the same as if you were to jump back into the ocean.

2. Only a Thought Away

Understand how close Heaven and your loved ones in spirit actually are to you helps in understanding how and why two-way communication with them is not as crazy as you may think!

Every living thing on this earth communicates with others, and this is done energetically and telepathically. Telepathy is communicating by means other than the five senses.

In other words, using the "sixth" sense...

Any thoughts you have cause brain waves, and these waves, which are energy signals, are received or heard by your loved ones in spirit. Now you may be wondering how on earth (or Heaven) it is that a spirit is able to hear your thoughts to them. Just think of your thoughts as a radio wave and those in spirit as the receivers, and vice versa. Spirits also give out this same energy signal, one you can receive. So remember when you think to a spirit (or speak to them out loud), they will hear you no matter if they are standing right beside you or doing what they are doing in Heaven.

I remember one time my sister Kathy (who is an author and afterlife speaker) and I were being interviewed on the radio by television personality Ryan Seacrest. Ryan asked us how it is that a spirit is able to find me. My answer to that question is that someone can pick up a cell phone and punch in numbers and speak to someone anywhere in the world ... let's just say Heaven's "technology" is somewhat more advanced.

You also may be wondering, if your loved ones and spirits are able to hear you loud and clear, why are you not able to do the same?

The reason for this is because they receive your communications to them consciously and you receive their messages and guidance subconsciously, meaning acting or receiving without one's awareness. The difference between subconscious and conscious is that subconscious things are taking place around you and you are unaware of it, whereas you know conscious experiences are taking place.

Communications with your loved ones in spirit happen every day, but most of the time you may not be aware of it. A good example of how you experience things subconsciously is music. You probably don't realize it, but you hear music every day without ever noticing it.

When you walk into a store or a mall, there is usually some type of music playing. When you're watching a movie or television show, there is always some type of music that is playing in the background. And why?

Because the music that is playing in the background is to help you to feel emotions that the store, show, or movie wants to convey and have you feel. And this is usually done with your subconscious. Now I bet when you've been in a store or are watching something on television and all a sudden a song comes on that you know and like, you actually hear the music playing. Because you recognize the song, your conscious mind clicks on and makes you notice the music. And after the song ends, you probably go back to shopping or paying attention to what you were watching and once again the music fades into the background.

This is the way it is when you connect with your loved ones in spirit. They are connecting with you and giving the guidance they are able to give, along with their love. All you need to do is open yourself up and notice it.

———

I will give you an example. It was a beautiful spring morning and I was sitting by the window taking in the beautiful scenery outside. After a few days of rain and grayness, the bright blue sky was a welcome relief. I could feel the warm rays of the morning sun filter through the blinds as my next appointment, Brendan, called me exactly on time for his phone appointment, which he had been anxiously awaiting. Although he had always thought there may be an afterlife, Brendan, not really having anyone close pass into spirit, never gave it much thought. That was until the love of his life passed away unexpectedly.

"Good morning, Brendan," I said, answering the phone. "How are you today?" I asked.

Brendan paused, then replied, "Fine, I guess. Well I'm a little nervous, to tell you the truth."

"Don't worry, those nerves are going to disappear in just a minute or two … I promise," I told him.

I began his session, as I always do, by explaining how a reading works. Of course, I make sure that the person receiving the reading also knows that during the session they are invited to ask any questions they have for me or for the spirit they are hearing from.

"So, Brendan, who would you like me to connect with for you today?" I asked.

Brendan said, "I would love to hear from my girl-friend, Ashley, if that is possible."

"Okay, give me a moment and let me see if she connects to me," I replied.

I took a moment, opened my senses, and concentrated on Ashley. It took only a few seconds for her to come to me and I could tell instantly not only how much she loved Brendan, but that she had a lot to say to him.

"She's here, Brendan, and let me tell you, this girl is full of personality!" I said.

Brendan became more excited in his voice. "She really is?" he asked.

"Yes, and I actually have to tell her to slow down a touch because she is speaking really quickly to me!" I said with a touch of humor in my voice. "I almost can't keep up."

"Wow, that's her," he said excitedly, "that's exactly how she was; she never gave me a chance to get in a word." Brendan replied. We all laughed at that remark, even Ashley.

As with all my readings, the first thing I ask a spirit to do, if they want to, is to communicate the way they passed into spirit. This is a good confirmation for the person receiving the reading to hear in order to know that I am connecting to the person they want to hear from. It usually also answers some questions the person receiving the reading may have. I have felt many, many passings, but once I relay the confirmation, the spirit will then take the feeling off of me.

When a spirit is communicating their passing to me, usually it is done by letting me literally feel what they went through. With Ashley, when I asked her to do this for me, she gave me the feeling of not being in any pain, but also that it happened quickly. I asked her to myself if this was some type of car accident and she told me that it was.

"Brendan, Ashley is letting me know that she passed from a car accident. Does this make sense to you?" I asked.

Brendan didn't answer right away and then replied with a crack in his voice, "Yes, that is how she died." After a pause, he continued, "She was coming home and was in a head-on collision with a driver who had been texting." Silence filled the next moment or two and then he said, "The driver walked away, but Ashley was gone."

"Oh, I am so sorry to hear that," I said. I always feel for anyone who is suffering from the passing of a loved one, but it can be harder on those here when it happens unexpectedly.

"Well she wants you know that there was no pain when she passed and that she was in spirit instantly," I said to him.

"I'm so relieved to hear that," Brendan replied. "For some reason, I always felt that was the case." At that moment, Ashley also pushed hard to me that she had given Brendan a big hug, along with all her love, right after the accident took place. I knew where Ashley was heading with that message.

"Brendan, let me ask you something."

"Sure," he said.

Did you have a premonition or feeling that something was wrong the day Ashley was in the accident?" I asked.

"How did you know that?" Brendan asked, surprised. "Yes, yes, on that day, I felt something was wrong with Ashley, only to find out later that I had that feeling the exact moment Ashley had died." Ashley pointed to herself with a loving smile.

I said to Brendan, "Ashley herself was the one who told you. She is telling me that the moment she passed into spirit, she came to you and physically gave you a big hug and wanted you to know that she was okay. And at that time, you actually sensed her with you, which is why you felt something was strange.

"I did," he said, "I really did." I could hear relief in his voice.

I then told him, "She is also saying you knew that she did not suffer because she also told you this as well."

"Yes," he said, "Well I really thought this, but wasn't sure if it was just wishful thinking or not." I could hear Brendan sigh. "Is that really possible?" he asked.

"Not only is it possible, but highly likely," I explained further. "The moment that Ashley passed into spirit, not only did she continue to be with you, but she has actually been communicating with you since as well! She is telling me this is why you 'knew' these things: you heard her in your thoughts. Even though you may not have realized that it was in fact her telling you, it was," I told Brendan.

Brendan began to cry. "I loved her so much. Please, I want her to know this."

"She does, Brendan, and she wants you to know how much she loves you too. This is why you had and will always have connections with her. And I know these connections can seem to be faint, but remember, the more you are open to them, the stronger your communications with her can become."

"That does explain a lot," Brendan said. "There have been times I thought I felt her with me, as well as hearing her voice in my head. I just thought it was my imagination," Brendan replied.

With that, Ashley excitedly responded.

"Well Ashley wants you to know that not only have you been connecting to her, but *she* was the one who got you to make an appointment with me in the first place," I said with a smile.

"I can't believe this!" Brendan replied.

"Why is that?" I asked.

"Well I was passing time in a mall one day after work, when I walked by a bookstore. Now I do not read a lot of books, but I felt a kind of pulling feeling that I should go in. While walking around, I came across your book, *Never Say Goodbye*. The first thing that I thought about was that song by Bon Jovi with the same title, because both Ashley and I were avid Bon Jovi fans and loved that song. I said to myself, 'What the heck?' and bought the book. So, while reading your book, there were times I could swear I felt Ashley right beside me, telling me … 'that's right, keep reading, keep reading.' I felt that I should speak with you, so I scheduled this reading."

I replied, "It sounds to me as if Ashley got you into that bookstore to help you on your journey to understanding your own continuing connections with her. I think it's wonderful how she just confirmed the different things that you have been experiencing and feeling and that it has in fact been her that has been guiding you through this transition and on your journey."

"You're right, it's always nice to 'think' something is happening, but better now to understand and to know that it truly is," Brendan said. "This experience has truly lifted a weight off my shoulders."

Ashley continued her loving messages to Brendan, and after his reading, he knew to trust himself with any communications that he would be receiving from Ashley. He told me that he could feel her love for him during his reading and how that love would help him as he moved forward with his life.

People say I have a "gift," but what does that really mean scientifically? It means that I am able to receive communications from spirits not only subconsciously, but also at a conscious level. But even though I have a heightened sense of spirits and am able to connect more strongly than most, *everyone* in their own way is a beacon to spirit energy and is able to connect with loved ones in spirit.

If you think about it, anyone who has a certain gift— whether it is the best athlete, musician, artist, dancer, or really anyone who excels in their perspective field—even though they may have a true gift, they too still had to practice and work to bring out the best their ability had to offer. This went for me as well. Even though I have been connecting with spirits as long as I can remember, I still had to work at honing my gift in order to be able to have a two-way conversation.

So, my point is that even though you may not be the best painter, I bet you can put some color on a canvas and come up with something enjoyable. Or if you're not the best athlete, I bet you can still throw a ball. If you're not the best singer, I bet you can still hum a song. But if you try, the more you work at any of the above, the better you can become at them.

And the same holds true with your own connections with loved ones in spirit; I know the more you work at it, the stronger your communications with them will be!

3. THE PHYSICALITY OF LOVE

As we've been discussing, everything has energy. This includes feelings, emotions, and, of course, love. Just as a cell tower transmits signals to your cell phone, you too transmit energy that can be received and felt by another human being. And just as you can receive thoughts from those in spirit, you also can receive their emotions and feelings as well.

Most people think that when they feel they are loved by another person, it is only because that person tells them so, and along with hearing it, the mind reacts, therefore creating that "love" emotion. Well part of this is true, but not all of it.

When you have feelings for a person, positive or negative, your body and soul sends out this energy signal that then can be received by the person it is for. It would then be up to that person to be open to receiving that energy. It really does have to do with emotions, physics, and science.

When I am giving a reading, one of the ways a spirit will communicate their thoughts about the person receiving the message is through their feelings. Do they tell me how they feel about that person? Yes, but along with their words, their true emotions for that person also become part of the message. I then sense and can identify what those feelings are.

Normally, I will feel love from a spirit, but then there can also be varying amounts or degrees of love that I will receive, which then I interpret to understand what kind of relationship the two people had and still share.

An example of this is that I will often feel a different, stronger love from, let's say, a mother to their child rather than a grandmother to their grandchild. But don't get me wrong, many times I will feel the same amount or the same strength of love from a grandparent to a grandchild. But in those cases, the relationship the two had was in fact just as close as a parent and child would enjoy. This also holds true if a parent and child did not have such a strong relationship; this love I feel will not be as strong.

If a spirit was not close to a person while alive on earth, this does not mean they are not given the chance to be so in spirit; they usually are. They will then give me what type of love they felt while they were here, for identification purposes of the relationship in the past, and then change it to a stronger love that is experienced now.

———

Cari and Mary were twin sisters who loved each other as much as they both hated their rhyming names. And all through life, they would always laughingly get on their parents because of this, but were so thankful that they at least were not dressed exactly alike.

Just like with many twins, there was a strong connection between the two sisters. They would finish each other's sentences and know if the other was in a happy mood or a sad one, even if they were apart, which for these two was almost never. And the strong bond the two shared in childhood continued into their adulthood.

As time went on, both Cari and Mary fell in love with the men of their dreams, married, and had children. And even though the two were now separated by distance, with a thousand miles between them, they could still sense and feel the connection they had always shared.

But then the unthinkable happened.

One summer day, while Cari was enjoying time at the beach with her family, she decided to go swimming while her husband and kids were playing frisbee on the beach. Unfortunately, she was caught in a rip current and drowned.

At that exact moment, Mary knew instantly that something was wrong. She didn't know what, but she had a sickening feeling that something tragic had just happened. She was devastated upon hearing the news. Not only did she feel that she lost a sister, but she also lost a part of herself as well.

As time went on and Mary was living her life while picking up the pieces, something unexplainable started to happen. She continued to feel Cari as she had before. Thinking this was impossible, and hoping it was not just her imagination, she swore to others in her family that she felt Cari was trying to communicate with her.

Trying to fill the hole in her heart, not knowing where else to go and having read my books, Mary decided to schedule a phone appointment with me.

I started the conversation. "Hi Mary, great to be speaking with you today."

Mary responded, "Same here, Patrick. I have been looking forward to speaking with you."

I went on and explained how I worked and Mary told me she wanted me to connect with her sister Cari. I took a moment, opened myself up, and found Cari was more than ready to communicate.

"Your sister is here and, first and foremost, I feel a very special sister bond between you two," I said.

"We were extremely close," Mary responded.

"Well you still are," I said. I could feel there was such a special connection between the two.

Then quietly to myself, I asked Cari how she passed into spirit. With that, she showed me water.

"Is there a connection between Cari's passing and water?" I asked. "Did she drown?"

Mary was silent at first and then I heard sniffling and she quietly answered, "Yes."

"She wants you to know that she did not suffer in the least," I said.

"I was going to ask her that," Mary replied, now crying. "We would always answer each other before a question was even asked," Mary said.

"Well again, that shows how close you both really were and are," I said. "Cari knows how this event has changed everyone's life, but also wants you to know that she really is alright and continues to be with you and the family."

"I am so happy to hear that," Mary replied.

I felt yet another burst of love from Cari to her sister. When a spirit repeats a certain emotion throughout a reading, they know that I will relay that as more than just an expression, but also a message as well…

"Mary, Cari is letting me feel the love she has for you yet again, and she is very strong at doing so. This is telling me from her that you do feel her from time to time."

"I do!" Mary exclaimed. "I feel her all the time with me, just as I used too!"

I said, "Well Cari wants you to know that the special bond you had and will always continue to exist."

Mary replied, "I am so happy to hear this! We always had such a strong bond, and ever since Cari died I have felt her with me!"

"Well this is what she keeps telling me now; she is confirming that you have been feeling her with you and it's not just your crazy imagination!" I said.

Mary said, "I've said those exact words to my family! I knew I wasn't crazy."

Cari responded quickly. "No wait, Cari is not saying you're not crazy, just not about feeling her presence!" I said. Everyone laughed at this.

"Mary, Cari is smiling and telling me that she is now younger than you. Was she older?" I asked.

"You could say that. She was three minutes older," Mary replied.

"Oh my, you guys are twins!" I said, excitedly.

"Yes!" both Mary and Cari shouted at me at the same time. I told them they answered at the same time and we all laughed.

"Well then, no wonder I feel such a bond between you two!" I replied.

"You better believe it," Mary replied. "Patrick, can I ask you a question?"

"Of course you can, Mary."

"Well before this phone call, I did feel Cari with me. And while I am speaking with you, I still feel Cari with me. Since she is with you, can she still be with me? Or is what I am feeling now just my imagination?"

I answered, "Of course you can connect and feel Cari with you at the same time she is speaking with me. They do this with the different set of physics available in spirit. Though hard for us to imagine, just think of it as two radios in separate places receiving the same signal from one station."

"I can kind of understand that," Mary responded.

I could feel an agreement from Cari with my answer and also, I could tell she wanted to show me something visually.

"Mary, Cari is trying to show me something. It looks blue ... wait, she is laughing and wants me to tell you she is wearing a blue shirt. I'm not sure what's funny about that," I said.

"I don't know." Mary responded. "Oh wait, I'm wearing a blue shirt right now!"

"Oh, I get it. She says she had it on first, but she took it off because you guys didn't dress alike," I replied.

"We didn't!" Mary exclaimed excitedly. "We never liked to dress alike."

"And she wants you to know you both still don't!"

Cari gave other messages to Mary, as well as emotional heartfelt messages to her husband and children whom she also continued to look after. She told Mary never to dismiss the connections she would be receiving from her as her imagination. She also wanted Mary to always share her experiences with their entire family so they would not think they were crazy for what they too would be experiencing.

———

So remember, love is not just an emotion, but an energy as well. And the more you are open to giving it not only to those who are with you here, but to those in spirit, the more you will be able to receive from those here and there!

4. Spirited State of Mind

It's easy to scientifically prove the five senses that most people have:

- Sight: we use our eyes.
- Smell: we use our nose.
- Taste: we use our tongues.
- Hearing: we use our ears.
- Touch: we feel with our bodies.

There is another sense people also have, but it is the one that most are unaware of, that being the sixth sense. The sixth sense is an intuitive awareness not of normal perception. Or to put it simply, having the sense of the unknown or those in spirit. And what makes the sixth sense different from the other senses is that it is not as outwardly prominent as the other senses.

With a healthy body, it's easy to experience any of the five senses without even thinking about it. As described above, these senses are connected to different parts of the physical body, which are experienced through electrical impulses from our brain.

So, the question is, would the sixth sense also follow in the same course as the others and can it also relate to the brain as well? This has been a question I have been asked many times and one that I really was unsure how to answer.

My personal belief is that the body and soul are two completely different entities, co-existing together. The soul is the real person and that energy runs the machine or the body. And once our bodies shut down or "die," the soul, the dominant source of who we are, will continue our life's journey, in spirit. And as of now, even though there is no "scientific" way to prove that the soul actually exists, in my opinion, I do confirm this, as well as the continuation of life, with every reading I give. But is there a scientific way to prove or to measure the sixth sense?

———

I was approached by a well-known specialist in the field of neurotherapy named Dr. Glenn Weiner. Glenn happened to be the father of the top radio personality in Richmond, Virginia, Melissa Chase. In the past, Glenn had heard my sister Kathy and me when we had been guests on Melissa and Jack Lauterbach's show, *Morning with Melissa and Jack*. Glenn had been intrigued when hearing Kathy and me and wanted to know if he could "map" my brain to see what is actually taking place while I give a reading.

At first Kathy and I thought something like this might be interesting to do, but I was unsure what the exact procedure entailed and if there would really be any results that could be physically proven. I know when I give a reading I have to really shut my mind off and then deeply concentrate on the information I am receiving from a spirit. So yes, I could sort of see where Glenn might be able to find that I am able to slow my mind down with his test, but would the results be anything more than any other person who can deeply meditate?

That was the question!

So, we decided to take him up on the offer and told him that the next time we were on his daughter's radio show, we would be happy to stop by his office to conduct the experiment. A few months later, we proceeded to Glenn's office, which happened to be just a few blocks from the radio station.

As we entered the building, Glenn, a tall man with a warm smile, was standing by his door and greeted us. Next to him was his lovely wife, Sandy, the person to whom I was going to give a reading during the brain scan. Once we sat down, their daughter Melissa also popped in, as she also was extremely excited to watch what was about to take place.

Glenn then began to explain to us what the test was going to involve…

First, I would need to place what looked like a rubber swimmer's cap on top of my head, the only difference being that this had about twenty probes with wires sticking out of it. I thought that either this thing was going to electrocute me or I was leaving with a bad perm. Glenn assured me it was quite safe, and neither would happen. Kathy was in the corner taking pictures and laughing as she knew how funny my hair would look once I took off this cap.

He wanted to measure or map my brain at different states of consciousness. To do this, the probes would send out radio waves and these waves would measure different impulses taking place in my brain. The information being received through these probes would then be translated into numbers and graph lines as well as color imagery of my brain activity. Together, all this information would come together to form a scientific conclusion of my brain pattern.

Sounds simple enough, right?

After making final adjustments to the cap on my head, he turned on the computer and the first good news came through …

I did in fact have a working brain.

I told him that was good enough for me and I thanked him for the test. He laughed and said there was more. Glenn then proceeded to instruct me on how the test was going to take place. The first test or measurement he wanted to take was when I was at a "normal" state, this being how I usually am when I am not conducting a reading. I was instructed to keep my eyes open for ten minutes and then shut for ten minutes.

Trying my best not to move as I was instructed to do, I sat with my eyes closed. Of course, I did have to keep telling myself not to make a connection with spirits, so I tried to relax and think of a song I had just heard on the radio on our way over ... I believe it was the group Green Day, and then I went into some showtunes.

After the ten minutes were over, I was told I could open my eyes. Glenn proceeded with the next part of the test, this time with my eyes open and of course not moving. I decided that I would just look at another computer monitor he had, one showing nature pictures changing from one to another.

While keeping as still as I could and my eyes focused on the pictures changing on the screen, one photo came up of what looked like a close-up of a dead fish lying on its side in a pond. I know my brain wave must have jumped as I couldn't help but laugh and I had to ask why he had a dead fish as a picture? He and the group laughed too and said that the fish was not dead, it was only resting. Kathy remarked that not many fish rest on their sides with a blank look on their faces. But again, Glenn was laughing, insisting that's what it was.

So back to being quiet while I sat there looking at "the resting fish," waiting for the next photo to come up. And again, after ten minutes had passed, I was told I could relax. Then it was time for the good part, mapping my brain while giving a reading! Glenn asked me if I needed to take some time to meditate first before making connections with spirits. I told him that I did not, as I can turn "my gift" on and off at will.

As we began this next part, it was pretty much the same format as before. Eyes closed for ten minutes and opened for ten minutes while giving a reading to Sandy. I swiveled the chair I was sitting in and faced the rest of the group. Sandy, Melissa, and Kathy were sitting together, so when Glenn gave me the cue, I began the reading as I always do and asked Sandy what relationship she would like me to connect with. Sandy said she would like to hear from an old male friend and I then proceeded to close my eyes, instantly shutting off my mind and opening myself up for communication with spirit.

When I give a reading, although I will usually be able to connect with the spirits that person would like to hear from, of course, spirits are people too, and may have their own agenda. And although Sandy wanted to hear from a friend Harry who was in spirit, the person who wanted to speak first was someone different.

It was Glenn's mother, Louisa.

"I'm sorry, Sandy, but the first person wanting to speak is Glenn's mother," I said.

"That's fine," Sandy replied.

I continued, "Glenn, your mother is telling me that you are celebrating a birthday."

Glenn replied with a big smile, "Yes!"

"She's also talking about some kind of excavation taking place," I said. "Does this make sense?"

"We're doing some irrigation," Glenn replied.

"Okay, close enough," I said. "She's saying something about the cost of it and it's not going to be as bad as it seems."

"Okay," Glenn replied.

I continued. "Is there also a connection with clovers, or being lucky? Your mother is telling me this." While receiving this message I found it funny how strongly she was relaying it to me.

"Yes, we all think we are lucky," Glenn said with a smile.

With that, I felt a rush of energy, an extremely happy feeling coming from Glenn's mother. Although this also placed a smile on her face as well, I felt there was more to this message, but I continued on.

"Sandy, Glenn's mother is telling me that you two were not so close with one another," I said.

Sandy replied, "We were getting closer."

"Well she wants you to know she is even closer now to you and thanks you for looking after her boy, Glenn," I replied. This made everyone smile.

"Glenn, your mother is talking about fruit juice; are you trying to drink more of it?"

"Hmmm, no," Glenn replied.

I told Glen, "Well she keeps saying you are drinking some."

"I just drank some orange juice yesterday," he replied.

"Well that's what she is referring to, but make sure to drink more of it," I said.

Glenn agreed he would.

"She also is giving me pain in my chest; did she pass from cancer?" I asked.

"Yes, she did," he replied.

"Well she wants you to know that she is in perfect health now. She feels good!"

Everyone in the room smiled.

"Sandy, Harry is now here and is giving me a sense that you two were more than just friends."

Sandy replied, "He was like a brother to me."

I said, "He also wants you to know that you are getting younger each day."

Even though she may not have believed him and pushed his compliment to the side, she laughed. All of a sudden, there was another female standing right beside him.

I told the group, "There is also a female with Harry, let me see who this is."

I took several moments to see if this person wanted to speak. At first, she was a little hesitant, but then came closer to speak to me.

"This female comes to me as a sister, did your friend have a sister who also passed into spirit?"

"No, he didn't," Sandy replied.

"Well this person is letting me know that she is a 'sister,'" I said.

"My sister, Cheryl?" Sandy asked.

"Do you have a sister in spirit?" I asked.

Sandy said, "Yes."

I laughed and replied, "Well then of course it is your sister! Cheryl is asking if you forgot about her already!"

"She would be hard to forget," Sandy replied with a smile.

I continued, "Well Cheryl is telling me that being in spirit, as well as now knowing everything there is to know, she wants you to know how crazy your family really is."

Everyone in the room all laughed and said how true that was.

I continued, "She also wants you to know she is with the family ... lots of family. And because of this, God gives you more patience when you're in Heaven."

They all laughed hard at that remark.

I continued, "Sandy, Cheryl is not calling you a hypochondriac ... but you're a hypochondriac." That got me laughing out loud, along with everyone else, as they looked at Sandy and nodded.

"Well she wants you to know you have nothing to fear but fear itself. And if you knew what it was really like in spirit, you would want to be there today. But don't worry, none of you are going to be over there any time soon," I told the group. Hearing this seemed to please everyone.

With that, all of a sudden, I then received a message from her friend.

I said to Sandy, "Your friend Harry is asking if he's going to get another turn anytime soon!" I said, laughing. Everyone also burst out laughing.

But then Sandy's sister continued with her messages.

I turned to Melissa and asked, "Melissa, were you just teaching your daughter how to make breakfast? Cheryl is telling me you were just doing this."

Melissa responded, excited, "I was!"

"Well she wants you to know that you would be surprised at who was watching you both," I said. This made Mel smile.

I added, "But she also is asking, with your wonderful daughter, who is teaching whom?" Everyone laughed.

"Sandy, Cheryl is also bringing up the fact that you have been taking your mother to the doctor."

"Yes, I have," she replied.

"Is there something she is continuously dealing with on a regular basis?"

Sandy replied, "No."

"Okay, I'm getting that she is," I said.

Sandy thought a moment and replied, "She's been having trouble with her teeth and been seeing a dentist about it."

"That's what she's referring to," I said. "She says even though it is ongoing, it's going to be better after a few more visits. Also, have you been having any trouble with your eyes or with some glasses?" I asked.

"I did have a problem with my sunglasses, but it was taken care of," she said.

I said, "Well she wants you to know that you have her to thank for that!"

Sandy, shaking her head, laughed.

I then felt Harry starting to push his way through again, wanting to speak.

"Sandy, Harry is back and he is showing me the number eleven. Is this number connected with him, like his birthday or his anniversary?" I asked.

Sandy said, "Not that I can think of. Well … that was the day he died."

Melissa responded, exasperated with her mother, shouting, "Mom, that's what Patrick just said!"

That made us all laugh.

I continued, while feeling the love and affection Harry had for Sandy. "Well he wants you to know that there's nothing you've thought about him that has gone unheard by him and that he will always continue to look after you."

That meant a lot to Sandy.

And then of course, someone else started to come through to me, this time an older woman identifying herself as a grandmother.

I told the group, "There's also a grandmother here; she's telling me her name is Nanny or Nana, something like that."

Melissa excitedly responded, "Nana Dora!"

Sandy said, "That's my grandmother, Melissa's great-grandmother."

"Well Nana Dora has been looking after you too and is telling me something about you guys just being on a boat."

"We did, we just went camping and were on a boat," Melissa said.

I replied, "Well she was there too!"

Sandy asked, "Did she get on the turquoise boat?"

I waited a moment for her response, "No, she says she went on a dark one."

"Oh, the canoe!" Sandy replied.

I responded, "That's the one, she says."

I continued, "Melissa, Nana Dora is telling me that you are going to be teaching a class. Do you know about this?"

Melissa responded, "I've have been asked to teach, but haven't done it yet."

"Well she's says there's no rush, but in time you will," I told Melissa. Melissa nodded her head in agreement.

And with that, Sandy's sister started to speak again.

"Sandy, Cheryl is talking about your feet," I told her. Sandy started to laugh.

"It's something about shoes, or to be more precise, your feet … are you having trouble with your feet?" I asked.

Sandy looked at Glenn as if a secret had come out and said, "I have slight neuropathy in my legs."

I responded, "She says that's it!"

"Wow!" Sandy replied.

"She is telling me that maybe certain shoes or a massage could help," I told her. "She's showing me someone working with the pressure points of your feet." I told Sandy that this was not my field of expertise, but to check it out.

Sandy's sister then chimed in, "Make sure you wash your feet when you go." We all laughed.

Several other messages from each of their loved ones came through and then it was time to wrap up the brain-mapping session. Melissa was amazed by the information that came through, and Sandy was a bit taken back by speaking unexpectedly with her sister. Although Glenn thought his role was only to be that of the experimenter, he was pleasantly surprised that his mother had shown up.

Glenn said that it would take several hours for him to run through the information that came through and wanted to know if we would like to wait around for the results. Unfortunately, Kathy and I were on a tight schedule, but told him we would come back and that we would be anxiously waiting to hear what he found out.

———

A few weeks later, Kathy and I went back to Glenn's office to see what he had discovered, and the results seemed to have amazed even him.

Again, greeting us at the door, Glenn was all smiles and showed us back to his office, where we sat down. He then pulled up the test results on the computer.

The first things we were shown on the computer screen were graphs with lots of lines and charts full of numbers. To Kathy and me, it was as if we were gazing at a bunch of hieroglyphs, none of it making sense to us; but to Glenn, who was able to read and dissect what all this information actually meant, this made perfectly good sense.

Glenn excitedly explained to us that the test results showed that when I was at a "normal" state, not giving a reading, my mind was also shown to be normal. I thought this was good news: I have a normal mind!

Glenn showed the test when I was in my "meditative" or "reading" state, and that result really surprised him! He explained that when people are in a relaxed state, the brain will make what are known as alpha waves. This is what places a person in a "relaxed" state of mind, allowing him/her to be more receptive, open, and creative and less critical.

He explained that people who are skilled meditators, such as Buddhist monks, can actually turn on alpha at will. To mine and Kathy's surprise, Glenn said that when I am in my "connecting state" or communicating with spirits, my brain was able to produce an extremely unusual high number of alpha waves.

That's pretty cool, I thought.

And the next set of test results Glenn found even more interesting and less explainable.

Glen explained that when a person is in a total unconscious state, not perceiving any external stimulation, the brain will produce what are known as delta waves. And to his surprise, while giving the reading, my brain too was showing a high level of delta waves.

So even though I am able to place myself into this deep state of consciousness at will (or as he puts it, my brain was showing to be offline), I am simultaneously still able to be actively engaged, alert, and even speaking.

To actually be able to do these things is inconsistent with being in a delta state, and yet somehow, I am able to manage to be in this state as well as an alpha state at the same time, while still functioning incredibly well! It is as if my brain can be fully awake as well as in a sleep mode at the same time.

So, the bottom line is that Glenn said when I am communicating with spirits, my brain activity is highly unusual. Hearing this news, both Kathy and I thought it was pretty cool to know that there was actually some scientific evidence showing something unusual taking place in the brain when one is connecting with spirits. Glenn seemed to also share our excitement as well!

I then asked Glenn, besides all this scientific stuff, what he personally thought about the reading I had given to him and his family. I always find it interesting to hear what a person of science thinks once they have received a reading.

Glenn smiled and said that he thought it was a pretty powerful experience. The funny thing was that although he knew going in that the reading I was to give was meant for his wife Sandy as an experiment, before we came, he had intentionally asked his mother Louisa to come and speak as well. So, when Louisa was the first one in spirit to show up, not only did this shock Glenn, but what she said in the reading was something that really took him by surprise.

When Glenn was asking his mother to come, he had quoted something to her that she used to say, something no one knew: "I was born with a golden horseshoe up my butt." And when Glenn's mother strongly told him in the reading that he was "lucky," he knew she was referring to that statement.

With that, in the most "scientific terminology" Glen could use, he said that specific confirmation from his mother to him was like a Michael Jordan three-point shot! We all laughed at his "scientific" use of words.

We then thanked Glenn for all the time and hard work he put in and he told us how much he enjoyed working with us. He also said that he was going to use my test results as a teaching tool that others in his profession could learn from.

How cool is it that science and Heaven can, in fact, come together? There is no telling what the future holds.

5. When We're Ghosts

One day, you, me, and all of us living in this physical plane will be in spirit. And even though it has to do with physics, when you step back and think about it, it seems kind of strange, doesn't it? With the work I do, people will ask me if I think a lot about death or if I am afraid to "die."

My reply is no, I do not think a lot about death, and I am absolutely not afraid to die. This is due in part because of my gift and the work that I do, as I know there is no actual death (and if you may or may not have noticed, this is why I never use words such as death, die, or dead, since there really is no such thing), rather an actual continuation of our life, in spirit. I know at that time I will be reunited in spirit with my loved ones, as well as able to continue being with those I love who are here.

And what I have also learned from the countless number of spirits I have spoken to is that being a "ghost" ain't such a bad way of living.

I was once giving a reading to a gentleman named Ben. Ben was a home builder who was as giving to others as he was talented at building. From huge homes to tree houses, Ben enjoyed working with his hands and creating something he would be proud of, and that others would enjoy.

Ben also had another love in his life, his husband Scott. Ben met Scott when Scott joined his company as a carpenter, and the two fell in love with each other working side by side. From dating at first to becoming a couple to finally getting married, the two created what they were most proud of—a strong relationship and a deep, deep love for each other.

The two enjoyed weekend trips to the beach and climbing rock walls on their days off. They both volunteered for charities to build houses for the homeless and never got tired of making the job site fun for everyone there. The two seemed inseparable. From the moment they woke up at the crack of dawn until they fell asleep in each other's arms at night, both were the happiest they had ever been. That was until the day Scott did not come home.

At first Ben thought Scott had just been running late from errands, but as the minutes turned into hours, he started having a sinking feeling that something was wrong. That feeling was confirmed when Ben received a call informing him that the love of his life had passed in a car accident. Stunned by the news, Ben just sat in the dark, in shock. He couldn't believe that it was all over in an instant.

From that moment on, Ben's life had never been the same.

Ben had always been a happy-go-lucky kind of guy who had a smile on his face and a helping hand for those who needed it. Now he was someone who was just living life day to day, wanting to hurry to get through the day, only to have to start a new day all over again. The routine of life was all he felt he had now. Grief was all that waited for him when he got off the job and went into the dark, lonely house.

A friend of Ben's had suggested that he speak with me. Ben's friend had previously received a reading from me and it had helped him through a very difficult time, so he thought that it might be beneficial to Ben. Several months later, he was ready for me to hopefully make a connection with his love.

I began Ben's reading as I do with all of them. "Ben, what relationship would you like me to try to connect with for you today?" I asked.

With a painful sadness in his voice, Ben replied, "My husband … Scott."

"Okay," I responded with compassion, "Give me a moment and let me see if he is here."

I opened myself up to see if Scott or anyone else was set to speak, and with the rush of his energy I was feeling, there was no doubt that Scott was there and had been waiting anxiously.

"Scott is here and is telling me he is ready to go!" I said to Ben.

Ben smiled and replied, "I hoped he would show up today."

I felt Scott's energy and emotions along with his message to Ben. Scott had so much love for Ben, and he was excited!

"Scott is telling me that of course he would 'show up' today; he's asking where else he would be," I told Ben.

"I don't know how this stuff works," Ben replied, almost apologetically.

I smiled and said, "Oh, that's no problem. Scott says he didn't know either, until he was there."

Ben tried to hide his emotions, but his love for Scott was just too overwhelming and he began to cry.

"That's okay, you can cry," I said to Ben, "I not only hear Scott's words, but also feel the strong love he has for you. You guys are making me tear up too!"

"I'm sorry about that. I didn't mean to," Ben replied.

"No, that's okay!" I said with a smile. "It's wonderful that you two share such a love for each other."

Ben replied, "I always will."

"And I can tell you Scott feels the same way," I told Ben.

Ben started to compose himself as Scott continued.

"Scott is giving me some type of head impact, as if his head was hit. Was he in a car accident or did he have a head injury?"

"It was in a car accident; not his fault, as I was told," Ben choked on the words of his response.

With that, Scott replied. "Well Scott is telling you of course it was not his fault; he could outdrive you with any vehicle!"

Ben smiled and replied, "Wow, we used to always argue who was the better driver!"

"Well apparently you guys still are arguing about it!" I said with a smile.

I could see that Ben was now starting to relax more and getting into the conversation he was having with Scott.

With a tearful smile, Ben said, "Well at least I wasn't the one who got into an accident!"

"Damn, that was a good one!" Scott replied back to Ben.

I had to admit, although I wasn't expecting to hear that, it was a pretty good comeback. We all laughed.

"Well Scott is telling me that, as you know, the accident wasn't his fault and that his skilled driving actually saved someone," I told Ben. Hearing this, I started questioning exactly what Scott was referring to, but Ben answered my thought.

"Scott was driving home that night when a deer ran in front of his car. There was another car coming in the opposite direction, which also swerved away from the deer, but was heading toward Scott's car. Instead of Scott impacting this car, he swerved away from it and hit a tree. The other car didn't even get a scratch on it," Ben said, with eyes tearing.

As he was describing the accident, I could feel the compassion Scott was feeling for Ben. I could also tell that Scott wanted to lighten the mood and add to what Ben was saying.

"Neither did the deer," Scott added with a smile. We all couldn't help but laugh at that remark.

I continued, "Well Scott is telling me that you know it was just one of those things, and although it's hard to understand, he knows that it was just his time to be in spirit and just the way it was going to happen." With that, Ben seemed to comprehend, yet was understandably frustrated.

"If that really is the case, why him and not me?" Ben replied.

I took a moment and waited for Scott to answer Ben's questions.

"Scott wants you to know that being in spirit, you really do understand the 'whys' of this life, and there truly are reasons for everything that takes place. One of the countless reasons we can understand is that his soul's growth needed to continue to take place in spirit."

"What does that mean?" Ben asked.

"Ben, the purpose of this life is for our souls to grow, which is done through the love we give as well as receive from others. But keep in mind, this growth continues to take place in spirit. With Scott helping you, guiding you, and, most of all, loving you, not only will he be helping you in life, but his soul too will grow."

Ben nodded his head in agreement.

"Bottom line, Ben, Scott is telling me that he is still going to keep you out of trouble!"

Ben smiled at hearing this from Scott.

At that moment, Scott began showing me something visually in my mind ...

"Scott is showing me a house. Did you just buy one? Wait, he is showing me more than one house, are you building more than one house?" I asked.

Ben answered proudly, "I'm a home builder, this is what we both did."

"Well Scott wants you to know that he is still building right beside you!" I said.

"So, is Scott really still with me?" Ben asked.

Although I knew the answer to Ben's question, I waited a moment for Scott to respond.

"Scott is saying he is with you today, tomorrow, and will be always. He also wants you to know that he is going to do whatever it takes to bring that cute smile back to your face!"

Hearing this made Ben smile again and he replied, "That makes me so happy and relieved."

"Scott says that's better!" I told Ben. "And keep in mind, he already knows what is up ahead and will be guiding you to make sure you stay in the right lane, just like he *didn't* do."

It took us both a moment before we caught what he said, and then we all started laughing again ... another good one!

I was really enjoying my connection and conversation with Scott; he seemed to have my kind of sense of humor and I always think laughter through tears can be the best kind of medicine.

Scott then changed the subject and started to convey something about ghost hunting, and I couldn't wait to see where he would go with this message.

"Scott is telling me that you two used to enjoy going ghost hunting. Is this true?" I asked.

This brought a big smile to Ben's face. "It is! When there was an opportunity for us to do so, we would go to haunted locations and see if we could somehow capture evidence of ghosts."

"Well Scott wants you to know that, being a 'ghost' now himself, it's not as bad as you both thought!"

Ben laughed. "I just can't believe he said that!"

"Why?" I asked.

"Because we would always talk about ghosts and wonder if they were poor lost souls or trapped somehow."

"He's telling me that the only way he would be lost is if he would follow your directions," I said.

Again, we laughed at Scott's remarks.

"Scott wants you to know that really is not the case. Not your directions, that part was true, but the part that ghosts are lost souls. He wants you to know that ghosts are just people, people who continue to live and to love those who are still in this physical world."

"Will he make his presence known to me?" Ben asked.

I answered, "He sure will! Spirits give signs and make connections with you every day. By understanding how this is done, you will begin to notice Scott more than you can ever imagine!"

Scott added in his two cents...

"And Scott is promising that he will be haunting you for the rest of your life!"

Ben replied, "I sure hope he does!"

Ben thanked me for his reading and told me that it will help him to face each day happier knowing that Scott is with him today, tomorrow, and always.

———

It's funny how the word *spirit* gives off such a positive con-notation when talking about what we become when we pass, and yet the word "ghost" produces more of a nega-tive feeling or thought.

The fact of the matter is, they both have the exact same meaning!

———

So, do I know I'm going to be a "ghost" one day? You bet I do, and I am not afraid about it in the least.

And you shouldn't be either.

We're all here living this physical life right now for a special reason, and one day we will all be "ghosts" having learned and become better for it.

PART 2
UNDERSTANDING THE GRIEVING PROCESS

In this life, I think you would agree that everyone, for the most part, strives to be happy. And even though such activities as reading books and watching our favorite movies and television shows, or even working on a hobby can be entertaining, it is actually the people, family, and friends around us that we love who really bring us true happiness. (Of course, it goes without saying that this includes our pets too!)

But on the opposite end of the emotion spectrum, there is one state that is never sought out or wanted, and that is grief. When someone you love and care about passes, especially unexpectedly, grief can hit you like a ton of bricks.

Grief, at one level or another, is a universal experience when someone we love passes into spirit, and it is not pleasant. Yet believe it or not, grief can be very helpful. By understanding the process and stages of grief, not only are you able to overcome it, but you can connect with your loved ones in spirit more strongly than you ever imagined.

6. LAYERS OF GRIEF

To begin, "grief" in itself is not just one emotion; it is a state of being that is made up of fractions of different emotions. It is layered with sections or fragments that combine to form the total emotional experience. Some of these emotions you may experience by themselves, others you may experience all at once.

It is important to understand that by breaking down what grief is and what you are experiencing, you can better control how it affects you and even how long it can last. So, although there are many layers, let's begin by separating grief into several of the most common emotions we feel when a loved one has passed.

SHOCK

First and foremost, if you were to learn of the unexpected passing of a loved one, the initial feeling you would likely have is shock.

When in shock, it can seem as if your entire body goes completely numb and your mind cannot comprehend what you have just learned. Of course, there are varying degrees of shock, from the very slight to the more serious, which can affect you not only mentally, but even physically. This depends on how well you knew the loved one, whether human, pet, or other, who passed, as well as how your body reacts to this trauma.

Slight shock is a natural response when hearing negative news, as it is a mental defense mechanism our mind uses to filter in and comprehend devastating events. It is similar to how our body uses adrenaline to ease physical pain we suddenly feel.

DENIAL/DISBELIEF

Along with shock, denial or disbelief can be the next emotion we experience.

When you learn about a loved one's unexpected passing, you may feel as if you have heard wrong, there is a terrible mistake, someone may be joking, or the news is simply not true.

This thought process and accompanying emotion will usually occur only for a few moments, until you learn more facts about the situation and your mind has time to decipher the information, categorize it, and react accordingly.

ANGER

It's is not unexpected or even unnatural to feel anger when a loved one passes, and there are several reasons for this.

- You may feel angry because you think the person has left you.
- You may feel angry for the way the person has passed.
- You may feel angry at yourself, for a number of reasons.
- You may even feel angry at God for letting it happen.

Anger can be an emotion that an individual uses in order to place "blame" on someone's passing. By doing this, they are able to "fault" or create a "reason" for the passing. Experiencing anger can also give the feeling of control over the situation, however false that concept may be.

DEPRESSION

Once the anger starts to dissipate, the next experience that usually follows is depression. This is what most people feel, and at times it can be quite overwhelming. There are countless reasons that bring on depression for someone whose loved one passes into spirit, but two of the principal factors are that you feel sad for the person who passed and/or you feel sad for yourself.

Let me give examples of both …

Sadness for a person who passed:

You feel sad for the person having passed after a long illness or from an accident. You feel that the person did not deserve this, or it was unfair for them to pass in that manner. You also see an inequity in the loss due to the character of that person.

You feel sad that a person's life was cut short. You believe that if someone passes when young, they did not have the opportunity to fulfill their time here and experience all that life has to offer. You view the loss as them having been cheated out of life's opportunities and prevented from realizing their goals and dreams.

You feel sad because you wish a person could have lived a better life because they were victims of negative circumstances or even abuse or violence.

Sadness for you:

You feel sad that this person is gone and is no longer a part of your life. You feel heartbroken because they are not here physically to enjoy life with you.

You feel sad that you can no longer make new memories with this person. You feel limited in the new experiences you can have alone. Having that person with you gave you the strength to try new things and go new places, but without them, you fear there are no new memories ahead.

You feel sad for unresolved negative past actions that you did not have the opportunity to change. You were always thinking maybe tomorrow would be the day to straighten things out, but now with their passing you think that can never happen.

You feel sad that you didn't let a person know how much you cared for them. You assumed they knew how much you cared, but you never really expressed your love for them. You feel cheated of that opportunity.

These, plus countless other thoughts, can bring on the feeling of depression, and the more you focus on these regrets or sorrows, the deeper the grief can become.

EMPTINESS

The feeling of emptiness is often experienced simultaneously with depression. An empty feeling washes over the body, as if something was taken from your soul, leaving a hollow spot inside. Other descriptions include:

- Feeling extremely lonely
- Feeling heartache, which can manifest in a physical pain or ache in or around your heart and chest
- Feeling a part of you is missing, like a piece of you is gone
- Feeling hopeless. Not seeing any future without that loved one beside you

This feeling of emptiness can give one a loss of purpose, an uncertainty on how to move forward.

GUILT

For many reasons, people find themselves feeling guilty about the passing of a loved one. This usually happens when a person blames themselves for something they did or did not do concerning the one who has passed. Some examples of guilt are:

- Feeling you did not do enough for that person
- Questioning yourself for how you treated that person
- Feeling you let that person down
- Having an argument with that person before they passed, without the chance to reconcile
- Not telling that person how much you loved them and how much they meant to you

Guilt can not only weigh heavy on the soul, but also on the mind. It can increase and encourage the state of grief because you feel that the past can never be resolved now.

HOPELESSNESS

Grief can also give you the feeling of hopelessness, which can have a negative impact in a variety of ways.

When feeling hopeless, you can:

- Feel suicidal, not wanting to live any longer
- Feel there is no future to look forward to
- Feel that all ambition is lost, with all hopes and dreams diminished
- Feel an extreme loneliness

Someone in this position will usually start to want to be alone and not associate with others. They can also feel that no one cares about them or understands what they are facing.

Tiredness

It actually takes a great expenditure of energy to be grieving, thereby making a person physically tired as well as emotionally exhausted. The fatigue associated with grieving can bring about the following:

- Feeling like you don't want to get out of bed
- Feeling like you don't want to leave the house
- Feeling drained and burdened
- Feeling unable to concentrate or think

When someone is experiencing this form of exhaustion, they lose all ambition.

So, as you see, there are many layers of emotions to grief, some or all occurring when a loved one passes. Have you ever experienced these things? I bet you have.

Most people will be able to work through these feelings on their own and/or with help from family and friends. But in some cases, help from professionals may be needed, as an outside person can listen to your situation and put things in perspective.

7. Going Through the Process

Now that you understand some of the emotions that cause grief, the next step is to understand and recognize how grief can affect you. Although grief itself is comprised of many emotions, there are also degrees to which it can be experienced, depending on the relationship you had with the individual who passed into spirit. Below is a breakdown of connections to a person and each association's degree of grief.

No Association

When you hear of someone who passed that you didn't know very well, maybe a friend of a friend or some other acquaintance, although you probably will not grieve, you more than likely will feel sad or sympathetic for those who were close to that person. The sadness you may feel with this passing usually will last for a very short time.

But you can also feel grief for someone you didn't know at all, someone maybe who was famous or well known. From actors, singers, and artists to even politicians, prominent figures do have an influence in our lives, and once they pass, there can be a feeling of interrupted purpose or an end to their work, which can cause grief. The level of importance this person's contributions had for you will determine how much grief their passing can cause.

Past Association

If someone you knew from the past is no longer a part of your life and passes—let's say an old friend you haven't heard from in years—this could take you to the next level of grief.

This type of passing can bring back old memories you made with that person. From the loss of childhood friends to old flames, these passings can bring the sense that a chapter in your life is now over and you are left with only the good times of the past.

This type of passing can cause one to reflect on what is lost with sadness, but these events are not usually life-altering and soon you are once again able to go about your daily routine.

Present Association

A passing that is disrupting or even life-changing is that of someone who was an active part of your life.

When a current friend passes, you can experience a deeper state of grief than those described above. This is because with this relationship, you did interact with this person, have conversations with them, and even associate with each other's family members.

It is hard when a friend passes, as not only do you lose the bond you shared with them, but their absence can leave you with time that is now no longer filled.

But there can even be a more difficult passing to experience, that of a family member. Although one day we expect the passing of our grandparents and then our parents, or even a sibling, this by no means makes the occurrence any less painful. When this type of passing happens, you will feel many of the emotions listed above, each holding a meaning that pertains to your relationship with that individual. You may also feel that you now need to assume that person's position or step into their role in order to maintain the unity or order of the family.

The next passing that will have a more personal impact is that of a spouse or a lover. This is someone you not only love, but are in love with. This is a partner with whom you shared your life, and without them, you do not feel complete.

But what could possibly be one of the hardest of all the passings is the one that usually comes unexpectedly, that of a child.

No parent ever expects to live longer than their child. When this type of passing takes place, even if it is expected due to the poor health of the child, it will be the most profound grief any person will ever know. This kind of grief changes a person, mind and soul. Someone who is going through this sorrow will tell you that their grief never heals, but they learn to live with it. And that is understandable. But what is important is how they choose to live with it.

Grief Time

When someone is in a grieving state, there can be specific times when the emotion can hit a person the hardest. An example of this is the time of day when someone who is grieving first wakes up from sleep. When a person awakens, it usually takes a moment or two to wipe away the cobwebs of sleep and to adjust from the dream world they have just been experiencing. When fully awake, the realization of the passing quickly comes back to the person, thereby setting off the sadness all over again.

Nighttime, as well as alone time, can also be especially hard for someone who is in a grieving state. After all the activities that may have filled the day are over, which often distract from the loss, one is then left alone with their memories of the person who passed, increasing the grief.

Not Wanting to Remember, Not Wanting to Forget

When grieving, thinking back on memories of that loved one can be very difficult. You find yourself wanting to remember all the good times you shared with that person, but at the same time, they can cause such pain and sorrow, and you believe there are no more memories to be made.

And then there are those memories you wish you didn't have. Perhaps an argument with that person, over something silly and forgettable, wasn't settled. Perhaps they needed help and it wasn't at a time you could offer it. These memories can leave one with the feeling of guilt from the past.

GRIEF TRIGGERS

There can also be what I call "grief triggers." You may experience these during this process. Grief triggers can be set off when you come across an item or a place that evokes a memory suddenly and without warning, increasing your feeling of grief. Sometimes when just walking around the house and finding a loved one's belonging, or driving by a special location that brings back their memory, you may experience a trigger of increased grief and it may add on an extra layer of emotional baggage.

Holidays, birthdays, and anniversaries are days that we usually look forward to. These are dates we celebrate with those we love and they hold the most memories for us. But once our loved ones pass into spirit, we may find that these days can no longer be enjoyed, which can make them the hardest times to get through. But there *are* steps to help move you through the grief.

8. Steps to Move Forward

Going though grief can seem like a muddy, slow slog, and moving forward can feel impossible. The more you break down the walls of grief, the stronger your connections with your loved ones will be.

Below are steps to help you relieve, and hopefully in time, lessen the pain you may be feeling. Remember, some of these steps will work out on their own, but the important thing is that *you* have to work on them as well.

Step 1. Time

As the saying goes, time heals all wounds. And although this statement is very true, some wounds are deeper than others, and therefore need more time to heal. When there is an "expected" passing, such as that of a grandparent or parent, there is a mental and emotional cushion that helps with the grief, allowing it to heal sooner than those unexpected passings.

When someone passes unexpectedly and without notice, it can take longer to process, as the shock can lengthen the grieving time. But no matter what type of passing you are experiencing, with the right mindset, you will find yourself on the right path in no time.

STEP 2. CRY

Release those tears!

Not only is it okay to cry when you are in the grieving state, it will help you! Crying helps you to confront feelings you may be suppressing. It also helps the body release negative feelings by lowering stress and elevating your mood. Think of it as washing out the sadness and letting the healing flow in. This will also help to lessen the sorrow you feel each time you have a memory of that person in spirit.

STEP 3. CONTINUE SPEAKING

There is nothing crazy about speaking out loud to someone you love who passed into spirit; it's even cathartic. When someone passes into spirit, usually the physical act of speaking to them also stops, which in turn causes a physical action in our life to cease. Speaking out loud can add a level of confirmation to our minds that you are connecting and communicating with those loved ones.

Yes, your loved one in spirit will hear you when you just think thoughts to them, but speaking to them out loud can help *you*, by giving you the feeling that the connection is actually taking place. Talking out loud mentally and physically validates the conversation and makes it more real from your perspective, which can strengthen the connection.

STEP 4. EXERCISE

Exercising is a great way to help you get through the grief you may be having! Exercising helps you concentrate on your body, taking your mind off your emotions. It helps to get your blood flowing and your energy up.

Now I'm not saying you have to go out and join a gym and work out with a trainer (although if that's what it takes to get you out of the house, so be it!), but even a simple walk around the neighborhood can do the body, mind, and soul good. And it will help you make a connection with your loved ones in spirit ... but we'll get into that later!

STEP 5. SOCIALIZE

Speaking of getting out, it's also a great idea to speak with people! Communicating is one of the best ways to help you get over that hurdle of grief. Family members, friends, and associates are usually the first ones you will encounter after a passing, and most of the time they will want to give you words of encouragement and comfort to help you through the sorrow. This will often lead to other conversations about your life and theirs and even help you to fill your calendar with much-needed future events. You may also be helping them fill their lives with activities and make new memories.

STEP 6. ADOPT A PET

It's important to express love, and that includes caring for pets!

Having a pet can help fill part of the void or the loneliness that can be overwhelming after a passing, while allowing you to continue giving and receiving love! Love is a real, physical thing, and just like grief, you don't want to keep it bottled up ... so give it away. You will not only be helping yourself, but a loving animal as well, who will give you years of unconditional love in return.

STEP 7. EDUCATE YOURSELF

Whether through books, the internet, or in the classroom, delving into the world of learning is an excellent way to help overcome grief.

By educating yourself, you will keep your mind occupied and alert, bringing opportunities that can lead you in a new direction. From meeting new people with the same interests to surprising yourself by learning something new, this step can make you feel like a whole new person! You can also teach others what you have learned.

STEP 8. GET A HOBBY

Yet another way to keep busy—which will help you with grief—is to develop a hobby. The good news about hobbies is that they can come in many shapes and forms. From gardening and painting to music and writing, hobbies usually consist of doing something creative, which in turn makes the mind focus on accomplishing a goal. Working on a hobby can fill you with a newly discovered passion, leading others to appreciate your accomplishments!

STEP 9. HELP OTHERS

There is nothing more rewarding than the feeling of helping others; just ask anyone who does this as a career; they will tell you how fulfilling it is to improve another's life. But you don't necessarily need a full-time career to gain the fulfillment that comes from service.

There are many opportunities out there that can put you in the position of reaching out. From volunteer work to participating in groups, your voice, your thoughts, and your opinions can help others at the same time as they are helping you!

STEP 10. BEING HAPPY AGAIN

The very last step to take and the one that can be the most difficult is to not feel guilty about being happy again.

As a person starts to reach the Other Side of the grieving process, guilt can rise up. You may think you are betraying a loved one, feeling it might be disrespectful to be happy or that the grieving period should last longer.

I can tell you through my many, many years of communicating with those in spirit that the number one wish they all want is for you to be happy!

As you know, a person who passes into spirit is not only in perfect health, but they continue to be with you, hear you, and see you; they are a big part of your life! And if the situation were reversed, would you not want the people you love here to be happy?

Of course you would!

Again, part of the "benefit" of being in spirit, besides getting to know what this life is all about and being in Heaven, is that they can continue to be a part of your everyday life too.

You know and they know that this "separation" (and I place that in quotes because you and your loved ones are only separated by physics, not by soul) is only temporary, until one day when we will all be in spirit. But until that time comes, it is important to live this life to the fullest and be as happy as you can, helping people along the way, while knowing your loved ones in spirit will always be by your side!

———

With each step you take, you are moving forward past grief.

Although keeping busy is important during the time of grief, as it can help you to pace and sort out the feelings you may experience without them becoming too over-whelming, it should not be a substitute for letting yourself acknowledge and experience the many feelings that may derive from the passing of a loved one. By suppressing such feelings, you could be delaying an experience that you (and your soul) need to go through in order to build a positive outcome by turning sad and devastating memo-ries into happy and joyful ones!

There is no time limit to the grieving process, as it is a road whose length is decided by each individual. But always remember that you will never go through it alone. Your loved ones in spirit are there with you, loving you and helping you through every step of the grieving process. And the sooner you get through it, the sooner you will be able to return to the happiness you once knew, united still with those you love.

9. Positive Side of Grief

So, if you are going through the grief process, you may be wondering, how can there be any positives? Well believe it or not, there are many positive outcomes from the grieving process; you just need to look for them. Remember that we are here in this physical realm for our souls to grow, and the passing of a loved one into spirit can help us with this growth.

The following are a few examples of how this happens.

First and foremost, you must remember that the relationship you had with a person in spirit can and does continue.

Your loved ones in spirit will always be with you, helping you and loving you. By simply having this mindset, you can strengthen your connection with them, as well as make new memories with them.

FEELING CLOSER TO THE SPIRIT

When someone passes into spirit, this will usually make the memories you have of them come flooding back. Just as if you were to run into an old friend you had not seen in a long time, and had forgotten how much you enjoyed them, you feel that joy return—this also happens with spirit. By remembering the good times you shared with someone in spirit, and even the love you have for them, knowing they continue to be a part of your life, the relationship you have with them will become even closer.

MAKING AMENDS WITH A SPIRIT

It's never too late to forgive and it's never too late to ask for forgiveness, especially with those in spirit. One of the biggest regrets I hear from people is that they never got the chance to ask for or receive forgiveness. With a passing, these regrets surface, coming to the forefront of the mind, and they can lead to grief.

But the good news is that it is never too late.

If you are struggling with this sense of futility, all you need do is reflect on the situation and know that person in spirit is there to ask for or give forgiveness to. By doing this, you can take a huge weight off your shoulders and release that burden forever!

MAKING YOU A STRONGER PERSON

There can be an inner strength that comes through the passing of a loved one. It's in the tough times that we learn, not only with our understanding, but more so with our emotions. Emotions and feelings are what drive us forward in this world, and the passing of a person can fuel your fire for life!

MAKING YOU APPRECIATE WHAT YOU HAVE

You know the saying "you don't know what you have until it is gone," and that certainly can seem true when someone passes into spirit. But at the opposite end, it can also make you appreciate those around you even more. It can bring gratitude into your life, and once being thankful is part of your everyday thought process, life becomes richer and more meaningful.

MAKING OTHER RELATIONSHIPS STRONGER

Passings can bring a family closer together. When a family member passes into spirit, this gives the remaining family members an opportunity to bond over the shared loss and the love they had for that person, strengthening the relationship they already have. But even though many families are not together, either from personal strain or geographical distance, a passing gives the chance for a family to reunite and become stronger.

GIVING YOU A NEW DIRECTION

Often, a passing not only causes one to recall memories with that person, but it can also cause one to take stock of their own life as well. This self-analyzation and evaluation can make clear where one's life is now and provide a vision of where they would like it to be. Having such thoughts and ideas can bring a renewal of hope for the future, along with the urgency and passion to go in the direction they now want to pursue.

HELP OTHERS GOING THROUGH THE SAME EXPERIENCE

When you go through the grieving process, you see that it is actually a journey, which hopefully you were given support to pass through. And by getting beyond the grief, you not only helped yourself heal, but you gave others around you the opportunity to grow.

Of course, these are only a few examples of the countless ways a negative can be turned into a positive. The actions I have described above, in my opinion, can bring you through the grieving process. If you are in that state, I hope this will help you too. But of course, there are many avenues out there, such as consulting therapists and physicians, that can also be helpful, so I suggest taking whatever opportunity feels right for you.

The fact of the matter is, grief is something that can be both physical and emotional. But the negatve feeling of grief can be turned into a positive, making you stronger than you could ever imagine, while allowing you to reach out and help others!

10. GRIEVING AND SPIRIT CONNECTIONS

Although the main reason for moving past your grieving process is to regain you own health and well-being, did you know that it can also improve your connections with loved ones in spirit? Believe it or not, it can. And having your own connections with loved ones in spirit will not only lesson your grief, but it can bring happiness back into your life, changing it forever!

Let me explain how grief affects your connection with your loved ones in spirit...

Have you ever noticed, when you go swimming, that the deeper you go, the denser the pressure of the water feels around you? This is similar to what spirits experience when they immerse themselves back into our set of physics to make contact with you.

As I have mentioned, when I give a reading, not only do I have to shut off my mind, I also have to "raise" my energy level. Spirits have to do the opposite to their energy; they have to lower it. With my energies up and theirs down, we meet somewhere in the middle, hence where the word *medium* is derived from.

On any given day, a person experiences many different energy levels depending on what is taking place around them, but most of the time it usually stays fairly even. Of course, when something exciting happens or you are feeling happy, your energy level goes up. But as much as we all enjoy that feeling of joy and euphoria, it only lasts so long.

The opposite seems to hold true for sad or negative feelings. It's all too easy to hold on to those feelings longer than others, especially when someone is grieving the passing of a loved one.

When someone is in a sad or grieving state, their energies are at a low or a slow vibration. This is where the saying "feeling down" comes from. And although this is an emotion, there is an energy that is experienced physically as well. But here is where the catch-22 comes in … The deeper the grief for a loved one in spirit, the lower the energy becomes, thereby making it harder for spirit to make a connection. And therefore, many times a person in such a state of sorrow may feel there is no connection with that spirit or that spirit is not communicating with them.

The truth is, being in a state of grief will put an invisible wall of energy around you, one that spirit finds difficult to break through. But do not be mistaken. No matter what lower state you may be in over a "lost" loved one, they are in fact with you. They see you, they hear you, and they are there to help you and (most of all) love you. Remember, just because you may not feel them with you does not mean they are not there. I assure you that they are.

PART 3
HOW TO KEEP IN TOUCH WITH YOUR LOVED ONES IN SPIRIT

It goes without saying that Heaven is an indescribably wonderful place, a place where one day we too will go and join those we love. But remember that your loved ones in spirit are not only *there*, but *here* as well, loving you, helping you, and guiding you in your daily life. The interesting thing about your everyday connections with your loved ones in spirit is that most of the time those connections go unnoticed.

The good news is that you can become more aware of these connections and communications from those in spirit, and by doing so you will utilize these signs in your everyday life, to help you with many aspects of your life's journey.

There are really two main ways you can make your connections with your loved ones in spirit stronger.

1. Understanding how the Other Side's connections are taking place
2. Understanding how you yourself can connect with those in spirit

By understanding these two fundamentals of communication, you will find your connections with loved ones in spirit are stronger than you ever could imagine!

11. Signs from Spirits

A "sign" from a spirit is something quite different. A sign is when someone in spirit will manipulate something physical around you so that you notice it. These signs come in many ways, shapes, and forms, but are usually very subtle. Remember, just as each of your loved ones in spirit are very different, so too can the signs be.

What is wonderful is that the more you understand the many ways your loved ones can send you signs, the less subtle they become, which will help you confirm their presence.

People receive signs from loved ones in spirit for many reasons, including:

- To assure you that the person in spirit is very much alive and well

- To bring you comfort in difficult emotional times

- To confirm that you are not alone
- To help in tough or even life-altering decisions

But remember, even though you may be ready and willing to receive signs, your loved ones can only give them to you when you are supposed to receive them.

Now you may be thinking, *my* loved one in spirit knows that I want a sign *right now* and they are going to give it to me if they *really* hear me and are with me. Well that would be nice, and they really do love you that much, but you do have to remember this: Being in spirit, your loved ones see the big picture about this physical life. They know and understand the full complexity of it, why they too went through all its challenges, and what their soul learned from it. They also know why you are still going through yours, and this is one of the greatest joys that Heaven brings to them: the ability to love and help you while you experience life.

By having this understanding, they also know that anything they may do can in fact change the course of your life. And this could unintentionally take you in a certain direction you are not supposed to go.

Let me give you an example...

Let's say you are at home, feeling sad and lonely, and you decide to go out and meet up with some friends. Sitting there, you ask a loved one in spirit to give you just one sign to let you know they are with you. As you sit there, all of a sudden you notice a light start to blink. It's never happened before and you are sure this is the sign you asked for. You get all excited and decide to put off meeting your friends and just sit there for the next few hours waiting for that light to blink again.

This may seem simple and not such a big deal. You just decided to wait for that sign one more time. But it may not be that simple.

What if you're sitting there for a moment and asking for a sign and it doesn't happen? You then decide to go out and meet your friends, and on the way, you run into someone you were supposed to encounter. And by meeting this person, you became acquainted with them and that leads you into a new friendship or relationship, perhaps even the ability to help someone in need, to take a new job—really, countless things could take place just because of the chance meeting.

But if you received that one little sign when you asked directly for it, none of the above might have taken place. And that could have changed the course of your life or someone else's.

If you are married or with someone you love, think back to the moment you met them. What one minor decision did you make on that day, or the day before, or the week before that placed you in that very position to know this person? That same concept applies to anything substantial that has happened in your life: a job, relationship, or anything else... it usually started out with one small decision.

On a personal note, when I think back on one of the biggest decisions I ever made in my life—to become a medium—I am amazed by how many things had to line up in my life in just the right order to bring me to that moment. If even one of them hadn't occurred, would I be a medium today? Makes me go "hmmm."

So remember that your loved ones in spirit will give you signs at the right time to enhance your life, not hinder it.

12. CATEGORIES OF SIGNS

Now that you understand some of the *whys* signs come when they do, what will help you as well as your loved ones in spirit is to know *what* you should look for.

As mentioned, signs from loved ones in spirit come in many ways, shapes, and forms. In the many years I have been a medium, not only have I noticed many types of signs from my loved ones in spirits, but I have heard of even more from people I have spoken with in my readings. Although I have mentioned some of the more common types of signs you can receive in my previous books, I wanted to include some here that you may not have thought about.

Thus, I have tried to "categorize" some of the ways spirits can give signs, in order to help you understand what you should watch for.

ENERGY SIGNS

Let's start with one of the most common ways a loved one in spirit will give you a sign, which is through "energy," manipulating everyday household items that use electricity or batteries.

Of course, one of the most well-known or common things a spirit can and will do is make lights blink or even a lightbulb burn out. Now I'm not saying that every time this happens it's because a spirit had something to do with it; sometimes it's just a bad bulb. But sometimes it's not, especially if you just asked someone in spirit to give you a sign!

Let's go over some other energy signs that you may not have considered.

Televisions

Spirits can be very tricky when it comes to televisions. I have heard from many people that if they are viewing a television show they watched with their loved one in spirit, the television may turn off or the volume may increase, and the channel may even change on its own.

So, if you asked for a television sign and your TV turns off on its own, that probably is your loved one letting you know that they too are enjoying the show! (Or maybe they are letting you know they don't like it, depending on what you are watching!)

As a side note, the funny thing is that this type of sign just happened to me! Just last night while I was watching television, my mind wandered off thinking about the different signs I wanted to mention in this book; suddenly, the channel I had been watching changed on its own.

It wasn't *really* on its own, as I then knew that I was being told to include this sign! Message received loud and clear.

Computers

Just like those on the Other Side like to manipulate televisions as a sign, spirits also like to have fun with your computers.

Sometimes not only will they turn your computer on and off and perhaps even make your screen totally blank, they also can change a webpage you are viewing.

And this next type of computer sign may sound strange, but stay with me...

You know those annoying ads you see pop up on a webpage from time to time? Well this too can be a message from a spirit. It's easy to get annoyed and just click off the ad, but next time this happens, pay attention to what the ad is about, as it can contain a subject or words that relate to a loved one in spirit!

And just as with your computer, routers can become lightning rods for spirits! Spirits can manipulate the speed of your internet service, causing your computer to slow down and even freeze up. If this happens to you, pay attention to what you are doing at that moment on your computer; there usually will be a connection (I mean that figuratively and literally) between that and the sign.

Digital Picture Frames

Many of us have a digital picture frame in our homes, displaying all the photos we enjoy seeing. Usually these photos remind us of the good times we have shared with family members, friends, and even our loving pets.

At times, spirits can manipulate the order of these pictures to have the frames appear in a certain order. And they can also make photos come up on celebratory days such as holidays and anniversaries. Also, don't be surprised if you think of a loved one in spirit, and suddenly their photo appears in the frame!

This can be a wonderful way for spirits to connect, as they also enjoy the old memories just as much as you do!

Digital Thermostats

A lot of us now have digital thermostats, and spirits can play with these too! There's an age-old belief that when a spirit enters a room, the temperature of that room can become colder. Well that may be true in some cases (not most in my experience, because if that were true in every case, the rooms I give readings in would be freezing! But I digress…) If this were to happen, it takes a lot of energy from a spirit to cause a person to sense them in this way.

However, due to technology, spirits are now able to take a shortcut! Spirits sometimes will change a room's temperature, cold or hot, by manipulating the digital thermostat, thus changing the temperature of a house. This happens usually as a sign to let that person know that a spirit is with them … or sometimes it's just that the spirit wants the house temperature more comfortable for them!

Bluetooth Speakers

What's becoming more and more popular these days are Bluetooth smart speakers. When these speakers are activated, you can direct them to play news, music, weather; really, the possibilities are endless, as the devices are connected to the internet.

Well that may not be all the speaker is connecting with!

Spirits can in fact make them turn off or on, have them play music on their own, even mess with the speaker's lights if they have them. If you own one of these devices, pay attention and don't be surprised if it goes off at times on its own.

Cell Phones

Have you ever received a message from an "unknown caller"?

Remarkably it may have been from your loved one in spirit!

Keep in mind, I'm not saying that every time this happens it is your loved ones in spirit reaching out to you with your cell; sometimes it really is just an unknown caller.

But if it happens while you were thinking about a loved one in spirit, if you are near a location that is associated with them, or it's a special day connected with someone in spirit, it could very well be them calling you!

Spirits can do this by manipulating your phone into thinking it is receiving a call, thereby translating it as an unknown source. Keep in mind, chances are if you pick it up and answer, you're not going to be able to speak to them directly using your phone, though that would be nice. It is just another way for a loved one in spirit to give you a sign that they are with you! I have also spoken with several people who have received a call and the number appearing on the phone was actually from a past loved one in spirit.

Again, this type of sign is not the most common, but one to keep an eye (and ear) out for ...

Music Players

Hearing a specific song can instantly take you back to a time and a place that puts a smile on your face. From the past to the present, music is the soundtrack to all our lives, able to transport us beyond our everyday circumstances. It can even act as an emotional reminder of a certain special someone.

This is why spirits love to give signs with music, which are usually instantly recognizable. From turning on the radio and hearing a song that reminds you of a passed loved one to even hearing lyrics in your head, spirits do have the ability to give you signs by music.

Most of us now listen to music with our cell phones or some other digital player. And although we use technology, spirits can still manage to manipulate these songs as well.

Try this next time you are listening to music on your device: play songs in "random" order, as there may just be a message in the way the songs are played!

Electric Fans

Believe it or not, even your everyday portable fan can be utilized by a spirit to give a sign. Not only can a spirit turn a fan on or off, but they can also change the speed while it is running.

I personally use a fan all the time; not only do I enjoy the feel of air movement in a room, but also enjoy the "white noise" it provides. The funny thing about white noise from a fan is that you really don't pay attention to it, but if it were to speed up or slow down, the sound usually comes to your attention immediately.

So make sure to listen up while staying cool at the same time!

Electric Candles

Candles have been around forever, used not only for light, but to give off scents, and of course to provide decoration. But with new innovations in the past few years, battery-operated candles have become even more popular than ever.

I own some of these and I tell you, with life-like flames that dance and flicker just as a real candle does, it can be hard to tell the difference between the two. And just as with real candles, spirits can also manipulate the battery-operated choice as well.

Of course, not only can spirits drain their batteries (it's a good idea not to ask for that kind of sign, as batteries can be costly!), but they can also mess with the candle timers, making them stay on longer or shorter than the time programmed.

So let the soft glow of the candle warm your house and this type of sign warm your heart.

Home Monitors

Many people now have home monitoring systems. Whether it's for home security, baby monitoring, or just to keep an eye on the pets, these cameras are now becoming more and more popular in our everyday lives.

But did you know they can also capture spirits? Well they can!

Many of these cameras have night vision capabilities and have been known to capture orbs, shadows, or figures walking around at night. If you do have the camera system that records constantly, you may want to review some of the footage, especially taken at night, as you never know what you might see!

Also, just like with other electronics, spirits can also turn these cameras on and off. If you noticed you have footage recorded for no reason, that very well could be done by your loved one in spirit!

Clocks and Watches

Even though everyone these days has a cell phone that shows the time and date automatically, people still use clocks around the house and continue to wear watches as well. I know I do!

And it's not uncommon to receive a sign from a spirit using a watch or clock; they do this in a few different ways...

- Making it stop running
- Making it run again after a period of time
- Manipulating the time
- Setting it to a certain date

Although some of these things will occur just because the battery went bad on its own, sometimes a spirit will actually drain the battery.

Not sure what I mean? Proceed to the next discussion on batteries...

Batteries

Speaking of batteries, have you ever replaced batteries or charged a battery in some device only to find that it has drained instantly? Well if this is something that happens all the time with a certain device, especially to a recharge-able battery, it really could be just a faulty battery. But if it only happens to the device every now and then... say hi to your loved ones in spirit!

Since batteries hold energy, spirits can drain the energy from them, and by doing so, can give a sign from whatever device that battery powers. Most spirits will usually not use this type of sign unless specifically asked. Most signs from spirits are appreciated, but having drained batteries is usually just annoying! (I know they are for me... and no, I cannot communicate with a dead battery!)

Kathy and I have gone on many paranormal investiga-tions when the batteries in our cameras or recorders will drain very quickly. Again, we ask for signs from spirits while doing these investigations, and this is one way they often provide them.

Remember, you might want to be careful when connecting something happening to an electrical item as a sign from a loved one in spirit, as many times these things can naturally happen on their own. What you do want to look for however is when these things happen at an unusual or specific time, such as birthdays, anniversaries, or when you are asking for a sign, so take note of the times they occur. By doing so, you'll know whether it's a loved one in spirit giving you an energy sign or not.

PHYSICAL SIGNS

Now a physical sign from a loved one in spirit can be quite different from that of an energy one. A spirit has to manipulate electrical current with energy signs, whereas they need to actually manipulate a material object for a physical sign by moving it or changing it somehow.

Again, some of the more common types of these signs you may already be aware of are pictures hanging askew on the wall or coins found on the ground, just to name a few; there are really countless ways a spirit can give this type of sign.

Here a few more physical signs you can look for that you may not have considered ...

Furniture Imprints

Spirits are still human and like to sit down and relax from time to time too! But being in spirit form, most of the time this too goes unnoticed by people; that is, until it becomes noticeable …

There are times when a spirit is in fact able to make their presence known by placing an imprint on a piece of furniture to show that they are with you. Let me explain.

When you stand up from a piece of furniture with a cushion, such as a chair, sofa, or a bed, you see an imprint from where you were sitting or lying. Well a spirit can at times also make such an imprint. The imprint is usually not as deep as the ones you make, but it can still be visible nevertheless.

Keep in mind that even though your loved ones in spirit are with you every day, and yes, may even be sitting there watching TV with you, this type of sign might only happen occasionally. Perhaps you'd like to put this book down right now and go check out your furniture, you may be surprised at what you find!

Furniture Movement

Spirits will also make furniture move at times!

Now when I say movement, I'm not talking about chairs being on the floor one minute and suddenly stacked on top of each other the next, such as is portrayed in the film *Poltergeist* (although that would be cool to see). When this sign happens it usually is extremely subtle, such as a chair being in one position and then having been moved. Or you may see something a little more noticeable, such as a rocking chair rocking on its own.

This actually happened to Kathy one time when she was a little girl. There was an old family rocking chair that belonged to our grandparents. It was used to rock us to sleep when we were babies, and now sat in her room where she would rock back and forth when listening to music or reading a book.

One night, she was awakened by the sound of that chair rocking, all on its own. But being the brave little girl she was (and still is), she got out of her bed, went to the chair and stopped it. But as soon as she got back into her bed, it started rocking again. She did not get up a second time.

Although these kinds of signs do happen, people can often be frightened by them; therefore spirits are reluctant to give them. But if you are open to this, let them know and you might just get what you ask for. But make sure you ask for it to happen in the daytime...

Wall Spots

It's funny the various ways a spirit can give you signs, and one of them can actually be leaving spots on walls. Most walls will usually either have paint or wallpaper on their surfaces, and spirits are able to manipulate the formula of the application, which in turn can leave a light or dark smudge like a shape on the wall. Sometimes the shape can even be a reminder of something meaningful to that person, such as a face, an animal, or even a place.

Now, if it rained or snowed hard and you see a wet spot on your ceiling, that's probably not a loved one in spirit; it's moisture leaking in somewhere. But if you do notice a faint spot and it reminds you of something, then it may be a sign. Funny thing, though, with wall spots: sometimes you can paint or wallpaper right on top of them and they will appear again!

House Noises

Some people just like to make noises, and this certainly can be true with some of your loved ones in spirit. Besides actually using the sound of their voices, spirits are often known to make other noises in homes.

With sounds like creaks, cracks, and bangs, spirits have a way of manipulating the physical attributes of a home structure to produce a sound. Now keep in mind, if you are hearing a pipe constantly rattle, I suggest calling a plumber. But if you hear a specific sound every now and then coming from your home, you're more than likely being haunted by a loved one in spirit!

(No worries … I am of course only kidding about the "haunted" part. As I've written in my previous book, *Always with You*, hauntings are usually just *your* loved ones in spirit giving you signs of their continued love and care!)

Misplaced Items

No, you're not going crazy!

Has this ever happened to you? You put down your keys, eyeglasses, or something else, and when you try to retrieve them, you find they are somewhere else. You think to yourself, "How did they get there?"

Well I'll tell you how they got there … a loved one in spirit moved them!

This is a harder sign to give, but a spirit can move an item from one place to another in order to make you look for it. And although this is can be just to give you a sign, it can also happen to place you in a position to look for that item so that you come across something else, or it even may delay you in order to prevent something else from happening.

Numeric

Now this is one I hear about from a lot of people, and I mean a lot!

Many times, people have numbers they associate with a loved one in spirit. Special dates such as birthdays and anniversaries are numbers that are meaningful to that person as well as to their loved ones in spirit.

Having these numbers tucked away in the back of their minds, people will often periodically see them throughout the day and be reminded of those loved ones they hold close to their hearts. From seeing the numbers on car license plates to numbers on signs and houses, or even on clothes people wear, they can be a sign from a loved one in spirit!

Now I'm not saying that your loved one in spirit placed those numbers on an item, but they can place you, or that item, in the right place at the right time for you to see them, thereby giving you another type of sign of their continuing love for you.

Physical signs are very identifiable once you and your loved ones in spirit know what you are looking for. You may have even experienced other signs that you were not sure came from a spirit. If this is the case, share your experience with others, as they too may have shared the exact same one!

ANIMAL AND NATURE SIGNS

A loved one in spirit can also give you signs with animals!

Through your loving pets at home, and even through wildlife, your loved ones in spirit are able to make a connection with animals and give you a sign of their presence.

Below are a few things to keep an eye on.

Pets

As far as animals go, we of course are closest with our loving pets, because as any pet owner can tell you, they truly become an integral part of the family. One thing about animals that you may not have realized, though, is that they are actually very sensitive to spirits. Since animals have the ability to see and hear spirits, your loved ones in spirit can use your pets to give you signs.

For instance, if you are a dog owner, have you ever noticed your dog barking for no apparent reason or staring out into a room at what appears to be nothing? How about a cat that is sound asleep and then suddenly jumps up and runs away?

Well here is the reason this may be happening ... your loved ones in spirit are more than likely teasing them! Keep in mind that spirits not only continue to love you, but also their pets here as well. They will still play with them, making them react not only to have fun with their pets, but to give you signs of their presence as well!

Birds and Feathers

Signs from birds are often ways a loved one in spirit will give you signs. The reason this is so common is because many people are already aware that they can receive this sign from those in spirit, and of course those in spirit know this.

One example of this sign is when you find a feather on the ground. Yes, birds do lose their feathers, and you may come across one from time to time only because of molting. The feathers you want to pay attention to are when one is perhaps in an unusual place, such as in your home, car, or even at a location associated with your loved one in spirit. Also, if you come across a feather on a certain memorable day it may be noteworthy.

You may connect seeing a certain species of bird with of a loved one in spirit. Perhaps seeing a red cardinal will instantly bring back thoughts of a loved one in spirit. Your loved one will then encourage a red bird to cross your path.

Again, my loved ones in spirit must be working overtime! I was just taking a walk outside with Kathy and discussing signs, when a feather drifted down in front of us. Perfect timing!

Other Animals and Insects

Although the previously mentioned are the most common animal signs, there are countless other ways that spirits can give these signs. From deer coming into a yard, to butterflies flying around you, spirits place animals in your path to put a smile on your face and to show their continuing care for you.

Open yourself up to this type of sign and you might be surprised at what you will receive!

Flowers and Plants

A less acknowledged sign, but real nevertheless, is a loved one giving a sign through plants or flowers. Just as with everything on this earth, flowers and plants too have energy. This is one of the reasons why when you are near them, not only may you notice their color and beauty, but they also make you feel good as well.

Well guess what. You may not have realized this, but that "good feeling" you are sensing is the flowers' and plants' energy! (And you didn't think you were psychic!)

Spirits are able to manipulate the energy of flowers and plants, making a flower last longer, or even having it change color. This of course goes for plants too, making one that may have been dying be revitalized and come back to life. Now don't leave for the weekend and ask your loved ones in spirit to take care of that old ficus plant that's on its last legs; that's your responsibility.

So, although this type of sign may not be easy to notice, keep an eye out on your flowers and plants as your loved ones in spirit may just have a green thumb!

Five Sense Signs

Although we will cover how you can use your "sixth" sense in order make a connection with your loved ones in spirit at a later point, I want to remind you that your loved ones in spirit can and will also use your other five senses to give you signs.

Spirits will use your sight, hearing, ability to taste, smell, and feel in order to make a connection with you. Of course, you will need to use your five senses in order to discern the other signs I just discussed, but spirits will use your five senses in specific ways to make their presence known.

For instance:

Sight

Most people will actually see their loved ones in spirit at one time or another out of the corner of their eye. But when they turn and see no one standing there, they pass it off as just their imagination. It really is not, though; there is someone who was and still is actually standing there.

When you have this happen to you, you are in fact seeing a spirit, but with your peripheral vision, which is also connected to your sixth sense. So, the key to this is not to turn your head, and you will notice your loved one in spirit standing there longer.

Hearing

Have you ever been thinking about a loved one in spirit when all of a sudden you have a ringing in your ears? If you have experienced this or even a high-pitched sound in your ear, this very well could be a loved one in spirit letting you know they are present, right there next to you. (But of course, if you are listening to music with headphones too loud, that's your own doing, and you shouldn't turn the volume up that high anyway, but I'm not one to talk…)

Ability to Taste

Ever had a craving for something at a strange time or wanted to eat something you usually don't like? How about having a taste of something that comes out of nowhere? This can be your loved one signaling for you to eat, or that they are hungry! Food can trigger many happy memories, from family gatherings, to celebrations and sharing recipes, and your loved ones in spirit know that this type of sign can remind us of our deep connection with them.

Sense of Smell

Another common sign from those in spirit is that of smell. A certain scent or odor, such as those of foods, flowers, perfumes, and numerous other items, can oftentimes be associated with a loved one on the Other Side, and they are able to produce it (you can say out of thin air), giving you that instant recognition of associating that smell to them.

Feeling

I'll bet there have been times when you have been sitting alone, either watching television, on the computer, or having a meal, when all of the sudden you feel an ever-so-soft touch on your arm, shoulder, or head. If so, you are sensitive to spirits!

This type of sign is usually more difficult to notice, but once you get the hang of recognizing their touch, you may be surprised by how often it will happen!

SIGNS CAN COME IN MANY, MANY OTHER WAYS

When you think about receiving signs, what I have just described are some of the ways you might notice when they occur. But remember, signs from a loved one in spirit are endless and can come in any number of ways, shapes, and forms.

I remember once when I was speaking with a man whose wife was in spirit. He mentioned to me that he had received one of my books from a friend, which had helped him in his healing. Of course, I thanked him for the compliment and told him I was happy that I was able to help him. During our conversation, he said to me that he had asked his wife, once she had crossed over, to give him a sign that she was fine. But he felt that the sign never came.

Or so he thought...

When I spoke to his wife, she said to him that she did in fact give him that sign. He was puzzled at first, but then she lovingly explained. She told me that her husband wanted to know she was fine, and by reading my book, he felt that she was. Her husband acknowledged that yes, after finishing my book, he knew deep down inside his heart that she was still alive and well.

She then laughed and asked him how he thought he came across my book in the first place? He replied that their friend gave it to him. She then revealed that it was because she was the one who influenced their friend to do so! She also said to tell her husband that he was as hard-headed as ever, that comment making him smile because she always told him that.

So, as you can see, signs can come in ways you may not expect or be looking for, which leads me to the question: How did YOU come about getting this book?

When looking for signs from your loved ones in spirit, never just look for the obvious, because more times than not, the coincidences you may experience or that luck you may have are actually signs from your loved ones in spirit!

13. RULES FOR RECEIVING SIGNS

So the big question is, what is the best way to connect and recognize the signs from your loved ones in spirit? By teaching you some of the rules when it comes to receiving signs, I promise I will help you make your connections with your loved ones in spirit stronger!

RULE 1: GIVE THEM TIME FOR A SIGN.

When you ask for a sign, can it happen on command?

Sometimes, but not usually.

There are many factors that determine when and where a sign can occur. As mentioned before, many signs that your loved ones in spirit give you go unnoticed. When you are trying to receive a certain sign, it may happen when you least expect it. If you remember this and are always open for that unexpected event, you will notice them occurring more and more.

Even though I am fortunate to be able to communicate one-on-one with spirits through my gift of mediumship, I still enjoy signs from my loved ones in spirit. I always tell them that when I ask for a sign, I'm not asking for myself, I am asking to help them not "get rusty." They of course know I like to keep them on their toes.

I recall asking my wonderful father (not during a reading, just in a passing thought) if he would give me an electrical sign in the next day or two. As I went about my day, even though I kept an eye out, I didn't notice anything that I would think of as a sign from him. But, after another week or so, something did happen. I noticed a lightbulb begin blinking and then stop as suddenly as it started. I checked the bulb to make sure it wasn't just loose, and it wasn't. I started to walk away and looked back again at the bulb. Sure enough, it blinked back at me. I knew this was my dad's way of winking at me, and yes, showing off. I thanked him and told him that he did a great job!

Later, when I was actually having a conversation with my dad, I asked him just out of curiosity why he was not able to do it within the following day or two after my request. He replied that he could, but if he had, *I* would have been the one to have "gotten rusty." Touché, Dad, touché.

In reality, there are countless reasons why signs come when they do. So, when you ask for a sign and it doesn't happen right away, just continue to watch for it, as it may come when you least expect it.

RULE 2: ASK FOR A "SPECIFIC" SIGN.

One of the challenges your loved ones in spirit face is determining what signs they can give you. A lot of people I come across tell they me that they ask their loved ones in spirit for signs all the time, but never notice any. When I then ask them what type of sign they requested, they will usually shrug their shoulders and reply, "Nothing specific, just any kind of sign."

Are you one of those people who ask for just any sign?

Well again, don't feel bad—most people do this, but that's why I am here to help!

The problem when you ask a spirit for just "any" sign is that you really don't know what you are looking for; therefore when they do give you a sign, you don't notice it.

Think of it this way:

If I asked you how many people yesterday you saw wearing something red, you probably couldn't tell me, because you didn't notice. But if I told you the next time you go out, count how many times you see someone wearing red, you then would know what to look for, notice it, and could give me an actual count.

So, you see, it's a lot easier to notice something specific when you are paying attention to it. And this is why it is important to ask your loved ones in spirit for specific signs. By doing so, not only do they know what you are looking for, you know what you are looking for too!

RULE 3: ASK FOR ONE SIGN, AND THEN TRY ANOTHER.

Now you may be wondering: what if you have asked for a sign, waited some time, but felt you never received it?

Well just like in this physical life, we all have certain abilities. You may be great at music or art. Perhaps you are good at cooking and creating new and exciting recipes. Maybe you are a wonderful public speaker. You see, we all have different strengths and talents.

The same goes for those in spirit!

When giving us signs, the Other Side uses a spirit's unique strengths and talents as well.

When discussing with people the different types of signs they receive, I find that most spirits can do such things as create bangs and creaking sounds coming from a house and move things about, or they can give electrical signs such as lights blinking on and off, or even mess with the television or radio. But to receive other individual and personal signs can solely depend on the soul and the ability they have to make that sign for you.

Although we can imagine what it takes for a spirit to give any kind of sign, you or I really do not understand the physics of what it takes for a spirit to give one. Again, whether they are able to give a sign through thought or if they have to manipulate the energy in this physical world, I have found that some spirits can do things special to them that others cannot do.

But don't worry, your loved ones in spirit can and will be able to give you some type of sign. This is why it is very important for you to know the optional forms, so you can experiment and acknowledge what your loved ones are able and willing to do for you.

So, if you have asked for a sign and do not receive it within a reasonable amount of time, simply ask for another type of sign.

RULE 4: DON'T FEEL GUILTY ABOUT ASKING FOR SIGNS.

I find it interesting how many people feel guilty thinking they are being bothersome to those in spirit by asking for signs.

Don't feel guilty! Never ever think you are a burden to your loved ones in spirit; you are not! In reality, you should feel the opposite, as spirits love it when you ask! When you are asking for signs from a loved one in spirit, this is actually opening up a discussion between you and them. You are speaking to them, and are then seeking an answer with the sign, making it a two-way conversation.

Any time you are conversing with a loved one in spirit, whether it is by asking for help, guidance, love, support, or even signs, it really does mean the world (this one and the next) to that loved one in spirit to hear from you.

RULE 5: SIGNS ARE NOT GOODBYES.

People have asked me if a sign from a loved one on the Other Side is a way for that spirit to say goodbye. My answer is of course not!

Remember, there are no goodbyes to those who love you in spirit!

Keep in mind, when a person passes into spirit, what those here perceive as the end, those on the Other Side know is the continuation of their life and their relationship with you. And as such, the people they were connected to and loved in this realm continue to be a part of their life in spirit as well.

Rule 6: No limits.

Once you receive a sign from your loved ones in spirit, don't be afraid to ask for more.

You must remember that signs from those in spirit are not only given to you for guidance or even fun; it's mostly out of love, and to tell you that they are still very much a part of your life.

Now I would suggest not getting hooked on them, meaning you stop living your life in order to receive signs. But if you live your life while noticing and enjoying the signs you receive, these will continue for your entire life!

14. BREATHE IN SPIRIT

Now that you are an expert on what to look for with signs, how about we focus on the next step of your connections with spirit…

Breathing.

As you know, it's always a good idea to breathe … right? Well if you don't think so, and if you are not breathing, there may be a good chance that you are already in spirit. But if you are breathing, keep reading…

Most people go through a whole day without thinking about the act of breathing. Taking in air and exhaling, going through the mechanical motions all day every day. Why? Because breathing is an involuntary body function that requires no thought.

I bet just by my mentioning it right now, you probably just started to pay attention to your breathing. Right?

But in the past, have you ever noticed how your breathing changes with your emotions?

On the average day, if you are healthy, your breathing is probably at a steady pace as you are breathing in and out, going about your day. But if you start doing something physical, let's say exercising for example, suddenly your heart starts pumping harder and your body needs to inhale and exhale faster, needing more air in order to keep up with its pace. Or let's say you are experiencing a heightened emotion, such as grief, excitement, or fright. Your breathing is affected as your body tries to react.

The examples above illustrate how your breath controls certain physical and even mental events you are experiencing. But did you know breathing can do so much more? Breathing the correct way can be a wonderful way to help you connect with your loved ones in spirit.

Using the right breathing technique can engage your mind and body to relax, clear your head from distracting thoughts, and raise your energy level. And clearing your mind can also help you to receive communications from spirits. As I have mentioned many times, spirits actually do communicate with you every single day, it's just that most of the time you are not in the right mindset or condition to notice it. I am happy to let you know that you can change this, simply by learning new breathing techniques.

The following breathing exercise will help to place you in the right condition, calming you and relaxing your body, thereby placing you in the right mindset for you to connect with loved ones in spirit.

ENLIGHTENING EXERCISE

To begin, if possible, play music, nature sounds, or white noise, as this can also calm you and prevent outside distractions as you are doing your breathing exercises. But if you are unable to have any background sounds, don't worry, you can still participate.

Now, close your eyes for the next minute, relaxing your body and mind, and simply take several deep breaths, breathing in through your nose and exhaling through your mouth. Do this step before you continue reading.

Now that you have taken in some nice deep breaths, I'll bet you feel more relaxed, don't you? Your body is not as tense and your mind is more open. So, as you continue reading, continue with breathing in through your nose and out through your mouth.

Repeat the above, but this time, as you sit with your eyes closed taking deep breaths, picture a beautiful, comforting, bright white light surrounding you. I want you to envision the bright white light now entering your body, filling you with all its energy and brightness. Do this now.

That wasn't so hard, was it? Even though you may have felt relaxed before, I'll bet you even feel more relaxed and more energized now. Congratulations, you just meditated!

Now I know that some of you may be thinking that this sounds ridiculous—making believe there's light around you and breathing the light in; that's just plain stupid.

Well I'm here to tell you it's not! There really is a science behind this.

By envisioning a light around you, your energies are challenged and your vibrations heightened, which in turn causes your body to react to these thoughts of calm and light. It's similar to when you are watching TV and you see someone eating something you love and you then crave it. You were not hungry before, but once your eyes saw the food, your body reacted by becoming hungry. Well it's the same when you "envision" something: your mind will react accordingly.

So, you can use the above breathing and visual technique for just a few minutes, or for as long as you wish. It can start your day off right, or calm you anytime you are in a negative mood, and also prepare you to make a connection with your loved ones in spirit.

15. MINDING SPIRITS

Meditations can be done in many ways, shapes, and forms. Most people shudder at the thought of meditating. I know I did. But once you understand how to do it, you will find it is not as hard as you may believe.

First, understand that there is no real right way or wrong way of meditating, just what works best for you. A lot of people believe that to meditate you must place yourself in some semi-trance and wipe out your awareness of the environment around you in order to be successful.

This is not true.

When I give readings, even though I must shut my mind off or even use a different part of my mind, I am still fully aware of what is taking place around me; the only difference is that I am concentrating on what I am doing.

An example of this is similar to when you are watching a television show. While you are enjoying your program, you are focused on what is on the screen, listening and paying attention to what you are hearing. But while you are focused on the TV, if all of the sudden someone comes into the room and begins speaking to you, your attention will then turn toward them. And once you have finished speaking with the person, you can then return your concentration back to what you were watching, actually going back into a meditative or highly focused state.

So, you see with the above example, you really do meditate or focus on things that you may not even be aware of, and this happens daily. When driving a car, walking, or even cleaning the house, your mind is in that meditative state.

When most people "try" to meditate, they will sit down quietly and try to erase all thoughts in their mind. The only problem with that is that when you try to tell yourself not do something, you usually will do it even more. The thoughts of daily life can come flooding in, making it hard to push them away.

But the key to meditation is to allow your thoughts to come into your mind, and when they do, experience them and then just focus back on quieting your mind. (Just like going back to watching television after an interruption.) The reason it is important to clear your mind is that it will help you to focus on the subtle ways spirits will connect with you.

These are some of the more common ways that spirits reach out to you, but that may go unnoticed:

- Give you a subtle touch on some part of your body
- Give you thoughts with visuals in your mind

- Send their voice so you "hear" them in your mind
- Send the sensation of their presence around you

Again, most of these things do take place on a regular basis, but they go unnoticed.

The good news is that you can instead start to notice them. By clearing your mind, you too can start to communicate with your loved ones in spirit through these connections. It's just a matter of changing your routine. Keep in mind, this is just like when you are exercising your body; the more you do it, the stronger you will become, and you will be surprised by your results!

MEDITATION EXERCISE

So, let's begin with the basics: relaxing your mind. First, if you have not done the previous breathing exercise, do so now. Now that you have done your breathing exercise and are relaxed, proceed...

Read each step and then close your eyes and do as instructed.

1. As you sit with your eyes closed, I want you to take a moment, and, as you steadily breathe, open yourself up to feeling the space around you. As you do this, you may feel a slight temperature change, as your body is now shifting and becoming more sensitive to the energy around it. Do this for a few minutes.

2. Now as you are sitting there (and remember to keep breathing!), notice if you feel any shifting or movement in the energy around you, similar to someone standing or moving about next to you. Do this for about a minute.

3. Notice if you feel any sensation on your skin, perhaps a slight tingling or even a gentle touch. Take a minute to see if this takes place.

4. Now I would like for you to think about a loved one in spirit; concentrate on someone you would like to hear from. Don't think of memories, although it's okay if you do. Just think about this person and then continue. I want you to envision that person actually with you now, standing next to you or sitting beside you. Go ahead and take a moment to picture this in your mind.

5. Wonderful, now that you are connected with this person, take a moment to give them a chance to communicate with you, which can happen in several different ways:

    Hearing: If you are hearing them speak with you, you may hear only one word or even complete sentences.

    Seeing: You may see the spirit or they may show you images in your mind's eye.

    Feeling: Once the connection is made, although the spirit can convey various feelings, the first thing you will more than likely feel is the strength of the love they have for you.

Remember there is no right or wrong way for what may come through, only your way and their way. So take a few minutes to absorb what is being communicated to you.

6. Now it's your turn. I would like for you to begin to speak with this person, and although you could do this out loud, I would suggest you "think" this conversation, as the sound of your own voice may bring you out of your meditation.

While speaking with this person, ask them any questions you may have.

Is there something you want to know about the past? Perhaps you would like to know how they are doing. Or, you may respond to what you just heard from them.

Have a conversation with this person, as the more open you are to this, the stronger this connection with them can be. Do this for the next several minutes.

7. Now, after speaking with them, it's time to end this connection. Although you can tell them goodbye, there are no goodbyes when it comes to your loved ones in spirit; they are going to always be with you. As you are doing this, not only listen to their words, but feel their emotions for you, as both will more than likely be a message of their love for you.

After you have completed this, it is time to open your eyes and reconnect with the world around you. Get up and stretch your arms, even walk around if possible, in order to release the energy and to get your mind back into focus.

———

It is not uncommon once you complete this form of meditation to think that you just have a great imagination and that everything you experienced was made up. Again, it's okay to think this, but this is where your loved ones in spirit will come into play.

While you are having a conversation with your loved ones in spirit, don't be afraid to ask them questions you do not know the answers to, or even ask them about your future or that of someone you know. Receiving this information from a spirit can give you confirmation that you are actually communicating with them one-on-one. And having this assurance will help to strengthen your connections.

Remember, if you expect them to give you the winning lotto ticket, you may be disappointed. But why won't they answer these types of questions?

Your loved ones in spirit are there to help you along your destined path, not change it. Of course that is unless you are on the wrong path or going in the wrong direction, then they can help guide you by giving you thoughts and ideas that can lead you back to the right road.

So embrace the love they send and always move forward knowing they are in your corner … every day.

16. Destination Meditations

Visual meditations are self-guided journeys that can take you to another place and time—with your mind—while meeting your loved ones in spirit!

The reason I like this type of meditation is because it helps me not to just sit and be "quiet," but guides me with visual thoughts that help me not to focus on the outside world around me. (It really is like watching television, only in the mind.) And by doing so, visual meditations help me increase my ability to have tunnel focus, thereby eventually making it possible for me to communicate with spirits at will.

So, I would like to share with you some visual meditations Kathy has created that we call "Destination Meditations," which I know can help you in making your very own connections with your loved ones in spirit!

The first is tropical beach meditation. This will take you away to a beautiful palm tree paradise as you envision the warm fine sands and the cool ocean breeze to set up the most perfect environment for meeting your loved one in spirit! Perfect for those who love the ocean!

The next is stormy night meditation. This leads you on a wonderful walk as you enjoy all of nature's magnificent surroundings and a pending thunder storm guides you to the safety of a warm, secluded special location where the energy of a storm will help connect you with your loved one in spirit!

Garden meditation takes you outside to your own backyard on a bright, beautiful morning. As you stroll around, you take time to notice all of nature's spectacular gifts and connect with that special someone in spirit!

And the last is coastal town meditation. You are invited on a seaside adventure where you will venture out not only to enjoy the sites and sounds of a beautiful coastal town, but to share the company of your loved one in spirit, with a special connection!

So, let's begin your wonderful meditative journeys.

Helpful Hints

To start you on your quest, know there are several ways you can proceed using destination meditations to begin making connections with your loved ones in spirit:

1. While you are reading a Destination Meditation, pause every now and then, close your eyes, and visualize what you just read as you meditate.

2. If you have a good memory, read a Destination Meditation all the way through and then visualize all that you just read.

3. Read a Destination Meditation out loud while recording it with your cell phone or an audio recorder, then listen back to it as you meditate.

I would suggest trying number 3, as this way you don't have to concentrate so much on the reading part and you can use it over and over again!

And before you begin, it would be a good idea to do all that is described in the previous section, Breathe in Spirit.

Keep in mind, you may have success with these meditations the very first time you use them, or it may take several attempts. But the key is to always trust any information or feelings you may experience during your meditation.

And remember, once you have completed any meditation, I would suggest standing up and stretching your body (you know, arms up, hands in the air, bending your body all around), or better yet, go outside and take a walk. Eating or drinking something is good also. By doing these things, you will remove any cobwebs in your mind that are left from your meditation and become more grounded back to this reality.

TROPICAL BEACH MEDITATION

What a beautiful day it is going to be!

As dawn begins to approach, you look up at the fading night sky. Only a few stars are shining now; the crescent moon is disappearing and the dark sky is slowly giving way to the dawn. You have found the perfect spot on the beach.

Sitting down close to the shore, you gently twiddle your toes in the white sand. What a wonderful feeling it is; the sand is cool from the cover of nightfall and the slight breeze beginning to envelop you is so welcoming and warm. Enjoying the sensation of the sand between your toes, you begin to notice the sounds of the sea. The gentle waves lap on the shore in a relaxing rhythm.

Gazing out over the pure turquoise water, watching the first sliver of sun beginning to rise, it's as if the small streak of subdued orange light has found its way into the night sky and is pushing it back to ready the world for the day ahead. As the rays become brighter, you begin to feel the warmth of the sun caressing your face as a new beautiful day is about to begin.

Sitting there, you notice the world around you starting to wake up from its respite. You start hearing the calls of approaching seagulls that begin to fly near you overhead. You look up and see two of them above in the sky, chasing each other as if they are playing tag together. As you watch, you smile, thinking how this morning could not be any more beautiful.

As you gaze over the ocean, the gentle breeze begins to blanket your entire body and you close your eyes to feel and hear all of the beach's wonder.

Concentrating on your surroundings, you take a few deep, cleansing breaths and begin to focus on someone you care about in spirit. As you are thinking about this loved one, you begin to envision this person coming toward you on the beach.

As they come closer, you stand up and smile while brushing the sand off of yourself. You notice that they too are smiling back and are happy to see you as well.

Meeting each other, you reach your arms out, as do they, and you embrace one another with a wonderful, loving hug. You deeply feel the warmth of this person and all the love they are giving you. Taking a step back, you look at your loved one and see that they are not only in perfect health, but notice a brightness and happiness in their eyes that lets you know they are completely fine.

Feeling completely relaxed and wanting to take advantage of such a beautiful day, you invite your loved one to take a walk on the beach. Of course, they smile, excitedly accepting your invitation, and you both begin your journey.

As you are strolling down the beach, you begin by asking your loved one how they are doing. You take a moment and listen to their response. It's so good to speak with them again, and you take in everything they have to say.

You then begin sharing things about your life, such as interesting things that have been taking place or people you've met. You see your loved one listening intently and smiling. They clasp your hand tightly, letting you know they have been watching over you and how happy they are now to have the chance to be with you here and confirm their love and their presence with you.

As the walk continues, you notice a perfect spot on the beach with a group of tall palm trees whose bright green fronds are swaying with the ocean breeze. You decide that this would be the perfect spot to sit for a while and continue your conversation with your loved one.

You see there is a large piece of bleached white driftwood that is nestled under the palm trees and decide it would make a wonderful bench for the both of you to relax on. As you sit, you feel warm and look up to see the filtered sunlight dancing in the shadows of the palms. You also notice how high the sun has become, as well as the beautiful, white, cotton candy clouds dotting the azure blue sky. You then turn to your loved one and decide to ask them questions about anything on your mind, such as life decisions or challenges you may be experiencing. As you are speaking with them, you notice how lovingly attentive they are as they listen, knowing how much they love you and want to help you.

Take a few minutes for this conversation to take place and listen to their loving responses to you.

You then continue the conversation with them, asking any other questions you may have and continue listening to their reply. As the conversation concludes, you both stand back up and stretch your arms out toward the sky, feeling all the energy of this tropical paradise around you. You then take each other's hands and you thank them for coming to visit with you today. You listen to their response, smile, and then hug each other tightly once more as you feel their love for you.

As they begin to walk away, they look back at you with that special gleam in their eyes and tell you that they look forward to coming again and are happy to be with you anytime.

You then turn back toward the crystal-blue water and watch the white caps of the ocean dancing on top of the waves as you reflect back on the wonderful visit you enjoyed with your loved one in spirit. It has refreshed your spirit and you look forward to speaking with them soon!

STORMY NIGHT MEDITATION

There is a warm breeze in the air and the afternoon sun is beginning to set to make way for the approaching night. You think to yourself, *what a wonderful time to take a relaxing walk and get your thoughts together*, and you step out on the front porch, breathe in the refreshing air, and head to the old dirt road down the lane.

The sun starts to move lower on the horizon; your eyes squint as the bright orange glow becomes stronger and shines between the branches. You feel the sun's warmth upon your face as it energizes your soul. Looking down, something catches your eye. It's a small green frog hopping across the road. As he stops to look at you, wondering who dares to trespass in his territory, he checks you out. Satisfied that you are not a danger to him, he hops off on his merry way.

As you continue down the road, the trees thin out a bit, giving you a clearer view of the sky, and you are surprised that the once-brilliant golden sky of the sunset has now been covered with approaching dark gray clouds.

Hurrying your steps as you venture further down the lane, suddenly you have the sensation of someone beginning to walk with you. It's a loving, familiar feeling that you are experiencing, and it is extremely comforting to you. A small rumble can be heard in the distance and all the green leaves of the trees now rustle in unison as the wind begins to kick up from what seems to be an approaching storm.

As fast as the storm is developing, you decide to seek shelter up ahead, as going back is not an option with as close as this storm seems to be. You remember that there is an old barn in the meadow a mile or so down the road and decide to take shelter there.

Small funnels of dirt from the road swirl with the leaves and create small mini-tornadoes that seemingly dance in the wind. Picking up your pace even more, you begin to notice a few sprinkles beginning to fall.

The small raindrops lightly hit the dirt at first, but they then seem to begin dropping faster and faster as the minutes pass. The night also seems to come quickly as the dark clouds enhance the dusk. Seeing the meadow just ahead, you rush through the field and the tall grass bends to your every step. On top of the hill just beyond the meadow you see that abandoned barn and seek shelter there.

Finding it not used in years, but sturdy just the same, you catch your breath in the barn and take refuge under its roof. The barn walls have boards missing, and through those spots you can see that the rain has begun to pour, just as the last light of day slips into night. You know you will be here for a while, and as you look around, you see an old wooden crate in the corner. You approach the crate and brush it off, placing it against the wall of one of the old horse stalls.

Sitting there, that feeling of someone with you is stronger than ever. The air is electrically charged from the storm outside and it makes the hair on your arms stand straight up. You make yourself comfortable on your wooden seat and relax. You close your eyes and now can see that the person you sensed with you is actually a loved one in spirit. This is someone you care deeply about and you are so happy to be able to spend time with them.

Take the time to really envision them in your mind. As you view them, are they at the age when they passed into spirit or do they have the appearance of being younger? Think to yourself how wonderful it is that you now have this chance to sit and converse with them.

You begin by speaking to them about some wonderful memories you two have shared in the past, and you go over remembered details that you haven't thought about in years. Some of the memories actually make you laugh and bring a smile to your face. It lightens your heart to remember the good times you shared. It's like a photo scrapbook in your mind. Flashes of wonderful experiences come forth, which strengthen the bond between you.

A loud crack of thunder shakes the ground beneath you, distracting you for a moment, but you know you are safe in this wonderful shelter. Looking out through the crack in the old door, halfway off its hinges, you see the rain coming down in sheets. The wind is howling outside and makes a small humming sound as it whistles through the cracks and crevices of the old barn.

A tap on your shoulder takes you back to your conversation with your loved one. You now begin to talk about your present life and all that is in it. How wonderful to confirm that your loved one knows what is going on with you and you feel such comfort knowing they are with you every day.

Taking a few moments, you become fully immersed in this conversation. You bring up all the challenges you currently face and you listen for their advice. You know they will guide you during this conversation and every day. The loving feeling and thoughts they share confirm you are loved. It has lifted your heart and given you a new outlook on life and knowledge on how to live it, aware that they are with you always.

The rain, which had been pounding the tin roof during your stay in the barn, has now slowed to a slight dripping sound. The wind that had been whistling through the wooden slats of the walls has now stopped and the leaves on the trees are no longer rustling.

You push open the door to find that the storm has indeed moved on. You look up at the night sky and see the full moon and shining stars emerging from what appear to be dark clouds, heading to their next destination.

You turn toward your loved one and thank them for keeping you company. You hold out your hand and feel a slight tingle as they clasp it. You know you will not be alone on the road home or on this road we call life.

Walking back through the meadow with the tall and now wet grass, you step back onto the dirt road. Although the dry dirt quickly absorbed most of the rain, large puddles still dot the road. The moonlight makes the night seem like day and illuminates the road ahead as the sounds of crickets and frogs begin to fill the air once again.

There is a freshness to the air as the storm has energized the night, and while walking home, you realize that the connections you have made will become stronger every day. And that brings joy to your heart and soul, just as it does for your loved ones in spirit!

Garden Meditation

You decide that today would be a beautiful day to spend some time outside enjoying your garden. When you are standing there, the bright golden beams of the sun begin to stream in through the window like a beacon of light, making a path for you to follow. You pull open the window to check the weather and you are immediately welcomed by a beautiful breeze that is pulling you outside. You cannot wait to take advantage of the invitation and hurriedly make your way to the back door and enter into the wondrous nature scene that awaits you.

As soon as you step outside, you feel the warm sunshine embrace your body and you lift your head up, close your eyes, take a deep breath, and enjoy the energy the morning has to offer.

As you look around, your eyes start to focus on your surroundings. The first thing you notice is that the picket fence you whitewashed last year now has a faded look you find pleasing. You walk up to it and see that one of the boards has come loose and you secure it back in place. This charming old fence seems to protect its surroundings, holding in all the beauty and framing it nicely.

You now notice that you hear birds chirping, softly at first but growing louder. You have heard this sound before and know that it can only mean one thing. They are hungry! You walk over to an old, slightly dented copper bird bath that has turned a bit green with age and has become a wonderful vessel to fill with seed. It confirms what you expected, as you see that it is now empty. You draw closer, and bright blue jays, brilliant red cardinals, and a small gray titmouse hover close in anticipation of the feast of sunflower seeds and peanuts that will soon fill the bowl.

You make your way down the broken, gray slate walkway, green moss growing between the cracks. The door creaks and sticks a little, as the wood is swollen from the last thunderstorm, so you have to pull with force until it pops open. It seems you have company, as many of the birds have followed you to the shed, knowing what lies inside. They sit on lower branches of the red Japanese maple that shades the front of the shed. You look up and smile at the chirping birds and tell them that you promise you will be right back with some goodies that will fill their tummies.

Stepping into the shed, you lift the lid off of the container and shovel several scoops of seed into a bucket. As you walk back outside again, the fresh air mixes with the sweet smell of flowers and with bucket in hand, you fill the bowl with the mixture. When walking away, you look back with joy at the birds enjoying their breakfast.

As you go back into the shed to return the bucket, you see small garden shears hanging on the wall. Taking them in your hand, you decide to go over to your flower-bed to pick out just the right flowers for the most perfect arrangement.

Walking toward your flowerbed, the sound of wind chimes catches your ear. The melodic tinkling of the glass sections hitting against each other puts together a symphony of perfect harmony. You take a moment and stand still in the beautiful sunlight just to listen to what the breeze is creating.

Continuing to your flowers, you see the newly opened buds from the many different varieties you have grown from seed. Periwinkle-blue bachelor buttons sway in the breeze as purple day lilies border the background. A small white trellis braces a beautiful climbing rose, where orange and yellow blooms abound. Each delicate flower is like a sunrise on the vine. Not only are the colors beautiful, but the aroma of each flower melds together on the breeze to make a floral perfume that dances on the breeze.

Taking your time and picking the ones that are just right, you snip each stem to the size that will fit in a sparkling crystal vase you already have in mind.

As you are gathering your flowers, you begin to feel the energy of someone with you. You know it is someone special, as you can sense this as a loving energy. Wanting for the connection to continue, you decide to sit in one of your favorite spots in your yard, on an old wooden bench that has valiantly stood the test of time and offers the most perfect view of all these magnificent surroundings.

You sit down and place your flowers beside you on the bench. Sitting there, you close your eyes, and taking a deep breath, you begin to feel the presence of that loved one whom you felt before even stronger, as if they were now sitting next to you. You open your eyes, and to your excitement, you see your loved one there, smiling back at you with warmth and love in their heart. You let them know that you are extremely happy to see them, and they reply the same to you.

You notice your loved one in spirit looks so heathy and vibrant. You tell them this and they nod their head to let you know how right you are and reply that there is a special glow emitting from you as well!

Now take the next few minutes to really converse with them. You are surrounded by all that Mother Nature has to offer, so use that wonderful energy that abounds to help with this connection. Talk about your life, your memories; really communicate with them and listen to what they want to convey.

Now, it is time to say goodbye, and as you do, you are filled with contentment and you smile at each other one more time as you close your eyes.

You start hearing all the lovely sounds rushing back to you from this beautiful meditative garden. The wind rustling through the trees; your wind chime continuing its song while the birds are chirping as if they were singing along to the sounds.

Taking another deep breath, you open your eyes and feel so refreshed by all of nature's wonders, but most of all, you feel all the love connections from your loved ones in spirit! You look forward to your next visit to your garden!

COASTAL TOWN MEDITATION

Looking out your window, you see the beautiful, light pink crepe myrtle in front of your window sway in the September breeze. The bark on the crepe myrtle gently peels away as the dark green leaves fill out the tall branches. On the tip of one or two of those branches, the leaves are just beginning to turn orange and yellow, hinting that autumn is just around the corner.

The summer season is on its last legs, but the temperature outside remains warm and slightly humid. Opening the window, you feel the warm breeze envelop the room as the metal hummingbird wind chimes hanging on the front porch match the breeze with a melodic harmony of soft tinkling. This beautiful day beckons you to come out and enjoy the last days of summer outside.

You decide to take Mother Nature up on the offer and go for a day trip to the coast. Putting everything on hold for just a day won't hurt and the excursion will energize you as well. When you step outside to go to the car, you see three squirrels chasing each other up and down the big oak tree that stands at the end of the driveway. The trio make high-pitched chirping sounds as they play. Around the tree like a barber pole stripe, they move fast, trying to catch each other in a high-speed chase.

Now in your car, you begin to drive, knowing this was a great decision and you cannot wait to see what adventures the day will bring. Within just a few hours' drive, you begin to reach the cute little coastal town and you follow the signs that lead you to the quaint downtown.

You notice that seemingly nothing much has changed in this town in a long time. Old cedar-planked buildings line the street. Mostly painted white, but weathered by age and salt air from the sea, the buildings almost look like a movie set from a New England seafaring film.

You park your car at the end of the street and decide to hit both sides and see what the folks are doing and what treasures you may find in these little trinket shops. As you begin walking, you also know your loved one in spirit will be on this adventure with you. It will be an adventure for you both.

You head down toward the waterfront. Instead of benches, there are large wooden swings that line the riverwalk. So inviting, you decide to sit on one and swing just a little to relax. Back and forth, back and forth, the rocking motion puts you in a calm state of being. You look out over the landscape where old wooden piers lead to small and large boats tied at the dock. They sway in unison with the waves.

Taking a deep breath, you exhale and it seems like all your stress comes out with it. It feels like you've left all your anxiety behind and your spirit is refreshed in this wonderful coastal setting.

You now begin to hear the sound of a boat in the distance as it blows its horn to announce its way into port. A chain that holds one side of the swing you are sitting in begins to make a creaking sound against the hook that holds it in place. At this time, you now invite your loved one to make their presence known, and it takes just a moment for you to realize they are sitting right next to you.

As the swing continues to gently swing, you begin a conversation with your loved one in spirit. Their happiness, excitement, and love is tangible, and being in this relaxed environment has heightened your senses. You start speaking with them.

As you begin asking your loved one questions, they softly respond. At first maybe just a few words, but then the messages come. You not only hear what they are saying to you, but feel each message with your heart as well. Your sense of touch is also heightened as you can actually feel the sensation of them sitting next to you, and even perhaps holding your hand. It's a warm, loving feeling and you just take it all in. They are a part of your life and this experience has confirmed to you that they have always been with you.

Take a few moments to really enjoy this connection.

You know that you will come back to this special place again, and realize that it's time to go back home. Spiritually embracing your loved one, you give so much love back to them. This is not goodbye but a continuation of knowing they are with you every day.

You get up from the swing, rejuvenated. Walking back up the dock, the sun begins to set on this special adventure. As you get in your car, you look back at this coastal refuge and know that the joy that came from this trip will be something you will experience again!

17. The Choice Is Yours

Your communication with loved ones in spirit really all narrows down to only a couple of things...

Either you believe in an afterlife and that your loved ones in spirit can and do communicate with you...

Or you don't.

And even though there are those out there who do not believe in an afterlife, no matter what, they will still have the love and support of their loved ones in spirit guiding them each day, even though they are totally unaware of this taking place.

The spirits know there will not be any communication from such a person, but if given a choice, they would like to have such a bond. Knowing the Other Side is there ready to help every day just makes the journey easier.

Sure, they know that one day that person will be joining them in spirit, and they will then probably be shaking their head and saying "I told you so." (You don't know how many times I hear this in readings ...) But the spirit still would like to have communication with that person here in this life. The same holds true with those who do believe in an afterlife, but think there is a disconnection from those in spirit.

I find it fascinating how many people who do believe in an afterlife feel their loved ones are still very much alive in spirit, but are disconnected from them. Again, if they don't see something, feel something, or hear something in this life, it doesn't exist to them, so they conclude that their loved ones in spirit are not with them and must be someplace else, a place called Heaven.

These people will usually think about their loved ones in spirit, and may even talk with them every now and then, believing maybe their messages will float up into the sky and be received by the loving spirits who have passed. And they hope to be reunited one day in Heaven.

Spirits connected to these people are present with their loved ones here as well; the only difference is that person here has put a "pause" on the relationship, and in their mind, think it has stopped until they too are in Heaven. Or, at best, they keep the relationship going with one-sided conversations with a loved one in spirit, not believing it can be two ways.

And then there are those who not only know that their loved ones in spirit are still very much alive, but they continue to be a part of their lives. And this truly is how one should live life with their loved ones in spirit! By having the understanding that life continues for a person who passes and that those in spirit are still with us, this will allow those in spirit, and you, too, to have an even more fulfilling life!

So, to conclude, it really is up to you how close you want to be with your loved ones in spirit. But always remember, no matter what, they will always be close to you.

PART 4
STORIES OF LIVING MY LIFE WITH THE AFTERLIFE

Everyone on this earth lives this life being loved, helped, and guided by loved ones in spirit. The only difference between myself and most is ... I am actually aware this is taking place.

To begin, there is a time when I am Patrick the "medium," and this is when I fully open my senses up and use my gifts as a medium in making a connection with those in spirit to help those here. Then there is also a time when I want to just be Patrick, and it is at this time when I am living life and doing things just like everyone else. And although I try to keep the two worlds separated, sometimes those in spirit have other plans!

I want to share with you some of these times, so you can get a real sense of what my life as a medium is like ...

18. COASTAL MEDIUM

It's no secret that I like to hang out at the beach. I've been lucky enough to live by both the Atlantic Ocean and the Pacific, both being unique and beautiful in their own ways, as with all oceans. I find there is nothing more cleansing to the soul than to just take a simple stroll on the beach, enjoying the ocean breeze, feeling the sand between my toes, and watching a magnificent sunrise or sunset … though really, any part of the day and night is wonderful on the beach.

It's no wonder some of my friends refer to me as the "Coastal Medium."

Although there are times when I like to find a secluded spot to just sit and look out into the distance and lose myself in thought and the energy of the ocean, I also enjoy being with family and friends, taking in the sun and surf.

I do recall one late afternoon when Kathy and I had finished a live event in Palm Beach, Florida, and decided to spend some time relaxing, you guessed it ... at the beach.

As Kathy and I walked on the sand enjoying the sights and sounds of the location, discussing the wonderful event we had given a few hours earlier, we heard a voice from behind us in the distance calling out both of our names.

At first we thought it may be someone who had also been at the event, but she wasn't familiar to either one of us. She came running down the beach waving something in her hand, and as she came closer, I saw that she was holding one of my books. When she reached us, she was out of breath and trembling. Kathy hugged her and then told her to catch her breath, and she began to calm down.

She told us her name was Rita and that she had so hoped to see us while we were in town. She said she was a big fan and she wanted to come to our event, but it had sold out. We told Rita that we were sorry to hear that but we were happy that she was enjoying my book, especially on the beach.

Rita seemed like such a warm person, and as we were speaking, I started to sense the spirit of her husband was with her. Of course, this did not surprise me, as I know how often loved ones in spirit are in fact right beside those they love.

"Rita, your husband is with you," I said.

"Well I always hope Benny is," Rita replied.

I said, "No, I mean he really is right beside you, talking to me."

With her eyes becoming wide, she exclaimed loudly, "He is?"

At that point, other people on the beach began looking at us.

I replied in a whisper, "Yes, but keep it down; you don't want all these other people's loved ones in spirit to know I'm here, because they will all want to talk too and I only have time to connect for one lady on this beach!" I said this with a smile on my face. She smiled back and blushed slightly.

I began to concentrate on Benny and receive his communications. Rita started to tremble.

"Benny is saying to me that you dragged him out into the sun today and he's not happy about it." I told her this in the humorous way Benny was relaying it to me.

Rita relaxed and laughed. "He never did like too much sun, but would go to the beach with me sometimes because he knew how much I enjoyed it. But Benny would always insist on sitting under an umbrella so as not to get sunburned."

"Well he's throwing a bottle of sunscreen away and telling me he's happy he doesn't have to worry about the sun burning him any longer!" I said. We all laughed.

At that moment, a Jet Ski whizzed by and the noise took me out of the moment. I had to take a deep breath and continue to concentrate on my connection with Benny.

"Benny is telling me that you're dying to get on one of those things," I said as I pointed to the Jet Ski, now in the distance.

Rita shook her finger at me and said, "He knows I've always wanted to give it a try, but he would never do it with me."

"Well he wants you to know that he's a bit braver in spirit and that if you do ever decide to give it a try, he will be along for the ride … and he means that literally!"

Rita replied with an almost defiant smile, "Well then, I may have to give it a try one day …"

"Benny is saying that he is so happy that you *know* that he is still with you and always will be."

"I do really feel him at times; not all the time, but sometimes," she said, her big smile fading.

"Well just know that even during the times you don't feel him, he is still actually very much with you."

"I do hope so," Rita said, as her eyes began tearing up.

I told her, "Benny wants to see that smile back on your face, and he wants you to know that he too is tearing up … but it's because of the ocean spray in his eyes."

We all laughed and Rita replied, "Oh Benny, you behave yourself."

I answered for Benny, "He says you know that will never happen."

That answer put the biggest smile on Rita's face.

"He would always say that to me."

Kathy replied, "You see, Rita, some things will never change."

As time was limited and Kathy and I had a plane to catch, we told Rita it was a pleasure meeting her and Benny and we hoped that she continued to enjoy her time on the beach, with him. Rita did email us a picture of her riding a Jet Ski, and I just know that Benny was along for the ride!

Here, although Rita was unable to join Kathy and I in our group, she just "happened" (I'm sure with the help of Benny) to catch us on the beach where her wonderful husband was able to bring through his messages.

I find it quite fascinating and wonderful how those in spirit can and will guide their loved ones, placing them in certain situations in order to make their presence known. Whether it is through any type of signs or actual connections, spirits will do this often with the ones they love.

Sometimes even if it means catching me on the sand…

———

"Spirit at Sea" is a cruise event Kathy and I like to hold from time to time. This is where we offer several different events on a cruise ship, including workshops, demonstrations, and other fun activities. Although these events take place on the ship, there is still plenty of time for us and our guests to embark and enjoy all the sights and sounds the islands have to offer.

On one particular cruise, we set sail to the Bahamas, and let me tell you, the majesty of the ship was only outshone by the beauty of the ocean waters. It also didn't hurt that the weather could not have been more perfect. The days were filled with beautiful, white, puffy clouds dotting the magnificent canvas of the blue sapphire sky.

On our first evening of the cruise we had a wonderful dinner with our group. It's always fun to meet people who have come from all over and get to know them on a more personal level. Later, by a moonlit pool, we ended the day with a nightcap and high expectations of the fun day ahead, which included visiting one of the beautiful islands awaiting us.

After one of our events, some of our guests from the ship tagged along with Kathy and I as we started our island adventure. After a nature walk around one of the most beautiful spots we had ever seen, we went to look at the different shops and markets around the island. Souvenirs and gifts hung from the rafters and I, with my height, had to duck most of the way through. Kathy did find several gifts for people back home, so it was worth banging my head into a few items … I guess.

After lunch, we all enjoyed the rest of the afternoon at a private resort where we had the privileges of its pool and beach area. The beaches are truly magnificent, with the bluest water imaginable gliding up to the warm, white-sand beach. After a short rest on the beach, Kathy and I decided to go on a quest to find some shells.

Kathy did not bring a hat, and with the sun being high and bright, it became bothersome to her. Making due, I took off my shirt and Kathy wore it on her head to shield her head from the sun. It was quite a sight and yes, I did take a few pictures and may have to share them on social media one day …

As we continued walking, I knew one of our guests from the group was going to join me in letting Kathy know what a "different" look my t-shirt on her head gave her, but she really wanted us to know how much she was enjoying the event. Hearing that meant a lot to us, as we wanted everyone in attendance to have as much fun as we did. We thanked her and told her we looked forward to the next event taking place later in the day.

As we continued walking, we came across a lovely older woman who was making necklaces for those who passed by and might be interested in a souvenir to take home. I could not pass up wearing a cool necklace. (Yes, I still have to be "cool," as you've read in my other books.)

We told her we both would love one and asked her name. She said her name was Jovana and we told her the beauty of her name reflected her beauty shining forth from her spirit. She gave us a great big smile. As she sat there working on my necklace, she asked us how we were enjoying the island, and of course I knew what was coming next … what did we do for a living?

I've gotten to know that when I answer that question and say that I am a medium, there will be a long pause and then the person will ask "A what?" or "Really?" In this case, it was "Really?"

As soon as I mentioned this to Jovana, I felt the spirit of a little boy with her. Again, even when I am, let's say, turned off, I will sometimes start to connect with spirits that are around people. I usually relay to the spirit that I am not connecting at that moment, but if they push themselves on me, that tells me I need to say something.

"There is a little boy here who seems very anxious to speak with you. Do you know of a small child in spirit?"

Jovana looked up from the work she had been doing and said, "I do, I do know of a small boy … he is my son."

Both Kathy and I replied "Aww" at the same time. We know that having someone you love pass into spirit is difficult, but when it comes to someone's child, that is the toughest experience a person can ever have, and our hearts truly go out to them each and every time.

I said to Jovana, "I believe he may have something to say to you, would you like me to speak with him?"

"I would very much like that," Jovana replied, with a bit of surprise in her eyes.

Jovana put the strings and beads down on her lap as I connected with her son.

"Jovana, your son wants you to know how well he is now and he is showing me that he's running and jumping in the water all the time!"

"Oh, that pleases me very, very much," she said, as a tear started to stream down her face.

"He was not able to run or jump or play like the other children," Jovana said. "He was born with muscular dystrophy and was bound in a chair all his life."

"I am so sorry to hear this, Jovana," I replied as I grasped her hand. "But he wants you to know that he is in perfect health now and he can even run circles around his mama!"

"I know he does!" Jovana said, smiling confidently. "My heart senses him around me and I feel him running around all the time. It means everything to hear you say this, to confirm what I've always known in my heart."

"And that is exactly why your son does this. It's makes him happy that you know this to be true," I replied.

With this, Jovana's son then showed me a tattoo he had. Although I thought he was a little young to have one, I knew he was just showing this to me as part of a message. He said to me that it was the one his mother had.

"Jovana, your son is now showing me a tattoo. Did you get one for him?" I asked.

With that, Jovana lifted her pant leg up and showed me a tattoo. It was a tattoo of a symbol, and when Kathy asked what it meant, she replied, "Life."

I told Jovana her son loved her tattoo and it made him happy that she knew that he was still very much alive.

Jovana responded, "I know that God has a purpose in this and I will be with him one day. I can't wait for that day, but one thing I learned with him is patience. I will be patient and just enjoy each and every day that God gives me here."

"That's right," I said, "while knowing your wonderful son continues and always will continue to be a part of your life."

Kathy and I gave Jovana big hugs. She hugged us back and there were tears from us all.

Jovana's son continued giving a few more messages and ended by giving his mother a great big hug too.

But before he left, he told Kathy and I that we had better get out of the sun before we began to burn. He laughed when he said this, and I know that part of the laughter was at my shirt on top of Kathy's head; I just know it!

Jovana, with a great big smile on her face, finished my necklace and then placed it around me, saying it was a "perfect fit. You and your special gift."

I treasure that necklace as a reminder of that special lady and the wonderful strength and spirit she possessed.

19. A Soldier('s) Story

One evening while "borrowing" Kathy's room because she had a nice stereo in it, I was looking at a book about a rich kid who was very well taken care of, by the name of Richie. Okay, it was a Richie Rich comic book, but a book nevertheless, and I was about eight or so years old.

While I was sitting in the bedroom alone, reading, I remember the feeling of someone looking at me. I didn't pay attention to it at first, but the more I flipped the pages, the stronger that sensation became. So, peeking above the comic book, my eyes perused the room. *Nope, no one here*, I thought to myself, and gave my attention back to Richie's adventures.

But still, there was that feeling.

After a few more pages, and that feeling still nagging at me, I slowly peeked over the comic book again, but this time, I saw what was giving me that feeling of being watched, and I will never forget it. There outside, looking through Kathy's bedroom window at me, stood a spirit, that of a Civil War soldier, peering at me.

Although I had seen other spirits in the past, usually relatives, this one was different. This was someone who was not related to me or anyone I knew. But what made this soul unique from any other that I had encountered in the past was how he presented himself to me. I had seen spirits who looked "normal"... well, as normal as a spirit can look. And by that, I mean healthy and happy.

But this soldier looking directly at me was completely different. First, I noticed that he was wearing a gray uniform and a soldier's cap. He had a blank look on his face, something I had not experienced before from a spirit, but the most shocking part was that he had blood dripping down from his head onto his face.

As I sat there frozen, unable to move and not knowing what to do next, Kathy walked into her room and my attention quickly turned to her; but then when I looked back, the soldier was gone.

Kathy asked me what I was doing in her room. I said to her that I was just hanging out there to listen to some music. But of course, I had to then tell her what I had just seen. As I proceeded, Kathy's eyes became wide as I described in detail that this soldier was peeking in her room and that his face was covered in blood. Kathy looked as shocked as I was. But to calm us both down, I told her not to worry, I didn't think he would cause her any harm during the night. Kathy then became angry at me, asking why I had to tell her all of this right before she went to bed!

Of course, being a kid and kind of enjoying it, I said to her I just thought she might want to know. Kathy did not sleep in her room that night.

Growing up in Virginia, I was surrounded by history. But for me as a young kid, this history was mostly taken for granted. When I saw fields and woods, these were just fun places I could explore and play in with my friends, but that was not the case when dealing with the ghosts from the past.

At the time, we lived next to a very old, beautiful oak tree, one with big limbs that almost touched the ground. Legend had it that President Abraham Lincoln and General Ulysses S. Grant climbed up that very tree to survey the area during the Civil War.

Just down the block from my house was a wonderful grassy field, and although it was completely flat, right in the middle of it stood a large, round crater.

As a kid, I would play football and baseball on this field and ride my bike on top of the crater, as well as slide down its hills on sleighs when it snowed. All the neighborhood kids did this. But the interesting thing about this crater is that it was not naturally formed; it was manmade.

You see, this field had actually been a fort, a fort that was created during the Civil War, built as a barricade to protect the soldiers during battle.

Of course, at that time, historical sites were not "preserved" as they are now (which is a wonderful thing), so to us it was just an awesome place to play. Thinking back upon it now, if we were to actually have seen the fighting and death that had taken place there, we might have thought twice about playing there ...

At that time there were no electronic devices or computers to keep kids occupied in the house, so we entertained ourselves the old-fashioned way ... we played outside.

I now reflect on how wonderful it was as a kid to be able to go outside, on my own, and find adventures to entertain myself each day. After meeting up with friends and taking a hike through the woods, or walking down by streams that wound their way to railroad tracks, I'd get hungry and then head back home to start these adventures all over again the next day. Each day brought a new adventure, while I never had to stray too far from home.

But with one of these adventures came a discovery in the woods that was totally not expected. One day while messing around in the woods, some of the older kids in the neighborhood discovered a location where a bunch of old bottles had been buried. These bottles dated back to the late 1800s and included vintage medicine bottles and many others. The bottles were all shapes and sizes and it was strange to see corks used, not screw tops.

As word got around about this discovery, more kids and even adults all went to dig up some of the newfound treasure. As the days went by and hundreds of these vintage bottles turned up, the spot was fully excavated, ending the treasure hunt, because nothing else was left to be discovered ... or was there?

Not long after, some of the older kids decided to go back and look around in the same location, but at a different area, clear of trees, in hopes of perhaps uncovering even more bottles.

But this time, it was not antique bottles they found. What they uncovered was an area of unmarked graves, and within these graves were several Civil War soldiers who had been laid to rest. Not only was this discovery shocking, but the news of this find spread like wildfire.

When I heard what was taking place, I remember running to the spot, as it was not far from my house. Once I arrived, there were already several adults there helping clear away some of the brush. As I came close, there in front of me was what had been discovered: human bones, now halfway uncovered from the dirt.

While I stood there watching what was taking place, I remember thinking about who these men might have been. I also remember feeling a sadness for them, as I knew they never made it home. Of course, the local authorities were called in, which led to the army coming to excavate the remains and rebury them in a historical cemetery.

Thinking back now on both of these events, was the soldier I saw staring at me through the window that night letting me know of the discovery that was ahead? Was he one of the soldiers that had been unearthed?

I may just have to ask him sometime...

20. Soul Sister

As I have written previously, soul mates are not only people you fall in love with, but can be people that you share an extremely close bond with, such as a friend or even a sibling who is a major part of your life. My sister Kathy is a soul mate of mine.

I feel very fortunate that I have Kathy in my life, not just as my sister, but also as someone I get to work together with. Not only has Kathy listened to or participated in many of my readings and shared her abilities, but together we both give live events where she will share her knowledge about the afterlife and her experiences of having a brother as a medium.

The funny thing is that although most people who know us think we agree on anything and everything in life, it really is quite the opposite. Let's just say there are many times when we act like a typical brother and sister, and sometimes our parents in spirit remind us of this...

———

Kathy and I were in London a few years back finishing up a week of shooting the TV show *Most Haunted*. We knew we had a day off and wanted to see more of England outside of London. We asked several people on the crew what would be a good spot to visit and they all agreed that we must go to Brighton Beach. Brighton is known to be one of the best beaches in England, and you know if there is a beach close by, I have to check it out!

The morning started off with typical London weather, cool and foggy, but gave way to beautiful sunshine. We hopped aboard a train bound to Brighton and were excited to see new sights. Riding the train, looking out the window, and passing the many townships and villages gives you a perspective of rural England. Sometimes it looked like a postcard, as small cottages dotted the beautiful landscape, while the different types of people would come aboard. All seemed excited to reach Brighton as the trained rolled on.

The beaches in England are not quite like the ones here in the states. Small rocks and pebbles replace the sandy shores we enjoy and the water temperatures are quite chilly.

Upon arriving in Brighton we exited the train with many other people who also departed. As we were leaving the station, we were not exactly sure where to go and how to get out of the station. It was a bit confusing to us as new travelers to the station. We noticed that people were holding their train tickets and using them to open and close a small automatic gate to exit. Easy enough, you would think … yeah, right. Evidently you have never traveled with us.

As Kathy and I approached the exit, we noticed one gate that was not being used and hurried to it in order to beat the crowds. Kathy, who was holding both of our tickets, gave me one and I proceeded to insert it into the machine, which opened the gate. That's where it all went wrong!

After I inserted my ticket, Kathy told me that I would need to wait for the ticket to come back through the machine before exiting, so that we would be able to reenter the station on our way back. So, doing as she instructed, I waited for my ticket to come back to me, but as I was waiting, the gate then started to close. So, at that point, I had no choice, I had to hurry past the gate as it was closing so I would not get trapped on the Other Side. But as I was running past it, the gate hit me around my waist area, striking my sunglasses hanging from my pants.

There, on the floor, now lay my sunglasses … broken in many pieces. As we were leaving the station to go outside, Kathy picked up the pieces of my sunglasses and took them with her. Anyone who knows me knows that I always wear sunglasses anytime I am outside, as my eyes are very sensitive to the sunlight. So having my sunglasses break just became a big deal for the trip.

Once outside and standing in a huge crowd of people, I was trying to shield my eyes from the sun with my hands, trying my best to adjust to the bright sunlight, when Kathy innocently looked at me and asked what had just happened. I told her that I inserted my ticket in the turnstile and waited for it to come back, but it never did. She then asked why I was waiting for a ticket, when she had our return tickets in her pocket? Now even more frustrated, I told her I was waiting for it because she told me to wait for it!

She, of course, then denied she ever told me to do so. I then asked her why else in the world I would have waited there unless she said to do so, and she replied that she had no idea what I was talking about, but had a guilty smile on her face.

Again, all of this discussion was taking place in public as people were walking by and looking at us arguing. Being six-foot-seven, I do stand out in a crowd, and people notice. The arguing didn't help, along with me not being able to see because of the sun shining in my face. I told Kathy, "let's just go."

So, as we began walking through the streets of Brighton, heading toward the beach, the sun now glaring in my face and me shielding it with my hand, Kathy started giggling, then broke fully into laugher at the situation. She turned to me with tears now streaming down her face, laughingly holding up the broken pieces of my sunglasses and told me I forgot my glasses and might need them. Of course, though I was a little peeved at the whole situation, her standing there with her hand out, offering my broken, unwearable glasses was quite funny. But I told her that it wasn't funny, while trying to hide my laughter from her. She continued making several more jokes, while holding the broken pieces out to me, and insisting that I put them on. Again, I told her, not funny ... but it really was.

Seeing that I was upset by not having sunglasses, she told me that, as a good sister, she too would not wear her sunglasses until I found a new pair for myself. You may think that was really nice of her, that she was standing in solidarity with me, but I knew better. I told her thanks a lot, but that it wasn't a big deal, since she doesn't usually wear them anyway.

As we started to explore the township in search of a new pair of sunglasses for me, walking down a street, I started to feel two spirits with me, our mom and dad. Continuing to walk, I opened myself up more so that I could hear what they had to say.

I happily relayed to Kathy that Mom and Dad were telling me they were with us, also enjoying the adventure we were on. That was nice to hear and we were happy they were having fun too. But then the conversation turned toward what happened outside the train station. They told us both, with smiles, that although it was a bit funny, we needed to behave ourselves in public; people had been watching us!

At that moment, we felt like we were both eight years old again. Laughing, we promised to behave ourselves and said we hoped they would continue to have a good time along with us. They said they knew they would; they always do.

It wasn't too long after that that I was able to find a new pair of sunglasses and actually see where I was going, allowing us to finally make our way to the beach and enjoy the rest of the day.

So even though we do act like brother and sister *sometimes*, we do love and care for each other *all the time*. And that's what having a soul sister is all about.

21. A HAUNTING
IN SAVANNAH

One of my go-to places that I love to visit as often as I can is the city of Savannah, Georgia. Savannah is steeped in rich history, and its tales of ghosts that are said to roam there are as old as the majestic, moss-covered oaks enjoyed throughout the city. The gorgeous old mansions and homes that line the many park squares seduce you back into another place and time. There is a strange and wonderful energy in Savannah, one that is like no other place.

I remember the very first time I visited Savannah. Kathy and I had just held several in-person events in Florida and decided on our way back to Virginia to stop by and spend a few days in Savannah while we were in the area. We had heard great things about Savannah, and since reading the book *Midnight in the Garden of Good and Evil*, and watching the movie of the same title, it was a place we always wanted to visit, so we decided to just do it.

When you go over the Talmadge Memorial Bridge that leads into the city, your first look lets you know that you are about to enter into a different time period. As you continue to drive in and look around, you begin to notice all of Savannah's charms as she invites you in with her palpable southern hospitality.

Once we were there, we decided to go ahead and park the car so that we could get out and stretch our legs and walk around a bit.

The way Savannah is mapped out is quite unique. The city of Savannah, Georgia, was laid out in 1733 around four open squares, each square surrounded by four residential blocks and four civic blocks. Each is unique and beautiful in its own way.

After visiting several of these parks, we ran across a cute little café named Clary's and decided to have a bite there. And although it wasn't a very large place, it was big in character. After finishing our lunch and heading out to pay the bill, we noticed several pictures hanging on the wall. Taking a closer look, we saw it was photos of the filming crew from the movie *Midnight in the Garden of Good and Evil* and that Clary's was used as a location in the film. We laughed because we had just recently watched the movie and didn't connect it to where we had just eaten.

Continuing our walk, we headed toward an inn we had picked out on our way to Savannah, the River Street Inn. If first impressions count for anything, by the looks of it, we picked out a wonderful place to stay. You see, the River

Street Inn is a 200-year-old converted cotton warehouse that sits alongside the Savannah River. And although it has been refurbished as a beautiful hotel, it still holds on to all its charm from yesteryear.

After we checked in, we proceeded to go through the beautiful hallways that display murals of the old south, deciding to take the steps in lieu of the elevator as we made our way to our room.

Opening the door, we were amazed at what we saw. Inside was a suite that looked like a room from an old southern plantation. Tall ceilings gave way to four-poster beds. Fluffy pillows lined the headboard and a cozy comforter covered the very inviting beds. The old brick warehouse walls were painted white, which added a brightness and cheeriness to the room. It also had floor-to-ceiling windows with great views overlooking the river below, and to the side was the bridge we had recently crossed to come into Savannah. A ship's horn could be heard in the distance, getting louder as it slowly made its way upriver.

As we stepped out on the balcony, we watched people walking up and down the old cobblestone street right next to the river a few floors below, looking as if they too were enjoying themselves. People leisurely strolled past the shops and restaurants, listening to the occasional street musicians playing music for all, taking a moment to stop and to listen. A cool vibe filled the air.

But as with anything else in Savannah, there was more than met the eye. As we started settling in and getting the feel for the room, a strange sensation from the room itself started to emerge. It was not a bad feeling, not at all. But it was one that gave me the impression that we were not completely alone in the room. And of course, that means only one thing: there were also spirits in the room.

Your first thought might be that as a medium, I would just open myself up and find out who was there. You would be wrong.

Again, there are times when I am Patrick the medium and there are other times when I am just Patrick. At that time, after a long drive and walking around the city … I was just Patrick! Talking with Kathy and acknowledging that she too felt a presence in the room, I decided to go ahead and grab a fast shower.

So, as I was showering, just down a small hall in the room, Kathy decided to rest her head on her bed. While lying there, the sensation of someone in the room started becoming stronger to her. Again, with how we live, we knew that there was in fact a spirit or spirits in the room, and she decided to speak to them just like they should be spoken to, like a physical person.

Kathy first thanked the spirit, whomever it was, for giving us the opportunity to stay at such a lovely location. She sensed that the spirit was not someone related to us, but may be connected with the building. When she asked this question of the spirit, the lights in the room blinked.

After I finished my shower, I came back into the room to find Kathy sitting in a chair. She told me that she had been speaking with the spirit and that the spirit made the lights blink for her. I told her I saw that too in the shower and wondered what was going on. Kathy said the spirits never seemed to rest and neither did she … that's why she got up from the bed and sat in the chair. It was part excitement to speak with new spirits and part "I don't want to be alone" to speak with new spirits. We both laughed.

So that night we had dinner at the Ladies & Sons, a restaurant owned by Paula Deen. This too is housed in an old building, and although it was kind of touristy, the food was good (*almost* as good as Kathy's!). After our meal, we continued our journey and decided just to keep walking around the city. Although there are a number of ways for tourists to see the city, from horse-drawn buggies to people-drawn buggies, we decided to continue walking and see what we could discover on our own.

After strolling around on a beautiful moonlit night, we came across a park bench just inviting us to rest our feet for a minute or two, so we did. Plus it would give us a chance to sit and take in all the beauty around us.

While sitting and discussing some of the sites we had seen and where to go next, I suddenly felt a male spirit approach me. I could sense that this spirit wanted my attention so, closing my eyes, I told him quietly that we could speak. It was time to be Medium Patrick again…

The spirit came through to me wearing vintage clothing and acknowledged that he was in fact the person who had been in our room. He said he was sorry if he had invaded our space, but he was so happy that we were aware of his presence. I then asked him if he was in some way connected to the room we were staying in or the inn itself. With that question, the spirit showed me an image of an old sailing ship. I then asked him if he had been a sailor on one that had been docked in the river near the Inn, and he held up a stone. This confused me. What is he referencing with a stone? I thought to myself. So, I asked him why he was holding up a stone. With that I felt a burst of pride coming from him and, as suddenly as he had come, he left.

Okay, that was strange, I thought. Not speaking with a spirit, of course, but why was the sailor spirit holding up a stone? Both Kathy and I had no idea what this meant. So we chalked it up to another mystery of Savannah and continued on our way.

When we arrived back at the hotel, with this mystery still nagging at us, we decided to ask the desk clerk about the ships that were docked at the river in the past. He confirmed that there were in fact boats there in the past, but there was a lot more to the story.

You see, back in the 1700s and 1800s, trade ships would cross the Atlantic Ocean coming from England to Savannah. These ships needed to be weighed down and stabilized by large stones, which would then be dumped upon arrival from the ships in order to make room for more goods from Georgia going back to Europe.

These stones that were dumped were then repurposed and used for building the streets, walls, and warehouses along the Savannah River, including the very spot where we were standing, the River Street Inn.

Hearing this, Kathy and I smiled at each other, knowing now the reason the sailor was holding up a stone. This spirit was proud that something as simple as the stones he once handled were now part of what makes Savannah a very special place.

That very first visit to Savannah has led to many more, along with other "hauntings." And every time I take a stroll on the streets by the Savannah River, I reflect back on that sailor, thinking that I may be walking on the very stones he once handled.

22. WATCH WHAT I ASK FOR

Just as I discussed earlier in this book, spirits can give many types of signs to show that they are with you, and I too enjoy receiving these signs. But there can be ways a spirit will give you signs you may not expect. And one of these came when Kathy and I were in Turin, Italy.

We had flown to Italy to participate in a paranormal investigation show that was broadcast live throughout the United Kingdom. It was a weeklong event with each investigation taking place at a different location each night. I was assigned to be stationed at the "hub," which was located in the city of Turin, on top of the Lingotto Fiat building. This was an important historical site in itself, as the building had been featured in different films, one of them being *The Italian Job,* and it was also located right next to the Olympic Village where the Olympics had taken place several years before.

Turin itself is a beautiful city. The stunning architecture and countryside made a living postcard. But Turin the city had a very interesting vibe or energy of its own. Each day, Kathy and I, along with the rest of the cast and crew, would be driven to an undisclosed location, one that was known to be haunted. We were never told of the location, and not knowing where we were going, nor the history of the location itself, made each trip quite exciting as well as intriguing.

Kathy and I do enjoy doing paranormal investigations, as we find that the spirits who "haunt" a location usually have interesting stories to tell. While spending time at each location, I would open up my sixth sense to see what type of history or occurrences from the past I could receive. When doing this, I can see visions of events that have taken place there, and feel the energy of what has transpired. And of course, I also open myself up to communicating with any spirits who may be present and want their stories known.

After spending time at a location, we would then head back to the hub and I would report back on television what I had encountered, while helping to narrate the paranormal investigations still continuing at the location.

Each day went like clockwork. We would visit a location somewhere around Turin, marvel at its beauty, investigate it, go back to the hub, and then I would share my experience live on television.

But one day, at a particular location, something was quite different about the place, but I just couldn't put my finger on it … at first, that is. This location was in the picturesque countryside. It was a centuries-old monastery, and from the outside (and inside) it seemed quite beautiful. With its cathedral ceilings and the intricate brickwork that is not seen in today's architecture, it gave the visitor a glimpse of a wonderful past.

As we walked around, getting the sense of its history, I felt its past start to come to life, and everything we were seeing in the present was not at all how it was in times past. Although I did connect with several good spirits that were there, I started picking up the struggles, sometimes violent struggles, that had taken place there—good versus evil, not in the biblical sense, but concerning the striving for power with nothing or no one allowed to stand in the way. What we were witnessing was just a mere façade of what had actually taken place there.

As I was describing this to Kathy and the crew, suddenly I felt a male spirit in our presence. I asked if he had anything he wanted to say, but no response came from him.

When I connect with a spirit, I can usually sense their personality and what kind of person they are, but not with this male spirit; he was not giving me anything, only that he was with us and he was watching us. Since he did not want to verbally communicate with me, I then asked this spirit if he would give some type of sign to show the others he was there.

With that request, the spirit left.

Okay, that was strange, I thought. Just the fact that this spirit made his presence known to me, but did not want to give me anything more than that was weird, or so I thought.

After we continued to investigate the property, seeing what else may come through to me, the sun was beginning to set and it was time to head back to Turin, to the hub for the live broadcast.

As we were driving back to the hub, in the car was Kathy, myself, an executive producer of the show, and of course the driver. About forty-five minutes into the drive, I felt something strange, or should I say, *someone* strange. It was that same spirit who connected with me just a while before. I took a moment to see if now he wanted to tell me something, but just as before, no response. Turning toward Kathy, I asked her if she also felt someone with us, and as soon as she acknowledged that she did, we heard a strange, loud hissing noise. We didn't know what exactly it was at first, but as the noise became even louder, it became abundantly clear what it was.

One of the car tires was going flat.

The driver pulled over to the side of the road and we all proceeded out of the car to see what exactly had happened. The front right tire was now completely flat, for no apparent reason. Unfortunately, there was not a spare tire in the car and as dusk began to filter in, we needed to get back before the show began. The driver had no other choice but to call for another car to pick us up. We waited on the side on the road, all of us looking at our watches as the time slipped by, until finally the second car did arrive and we were once again on our way.

The driver of this second car knew we were now in an extreme time crunch and that I had to be back soon for the live show. He drove as if we were in a James Bond film, weaving in and out of lanes, trying to get us there as fast as possible.

Once we arrived back, we were excitedly greeted by other show crew members who wanted to rush me right up to the set, as there were only minutes left before we went live. So, with seconds to spare, I was seated back on the couch, and while trying to catch my breath and compose my thoughts, I began smiling to myself, knowing what had just taken place. This was while I was being counted down by a cameraman, hearing, "five, four, three, two, one" and seeing the red light turn on, and being viewed live all around the UK.

A month or two after, Kathy and I were giving a radio interview and reliving this adventure. We spoke about how I connected with this spirit and how strange that although he had nothing to say, we asked for a sign, and it came, stronger than we had hoped. The hosts and the audience seemed intrigued by this and asked us many questions about our experiences.

But could the tire going flat the moment I felt the spirit with us in the car just have been a coincidence? Sure, it could have been, I guess, but then how do you explain what happened next?

Once we finished the interview and proceeded to leave, as we were walking out of the building, we couldn't believe what we saw. There in front of us was our car, with a flat tire on the front right side. Kathy and I just shook our heads and smiled. One, we now knew it was no coincidence and two, we did have a spare.

Again, always be careful what you ask for, because you just might get it ...

23. PLANE VIEW

It was an overcast drizzly day (or it was "spittin'" a little bit, as we say in Virginia) in Richmond, Virginia, when Kathy and I boarded a plane heading back to Los Angeles, California. We had a meeting with a television production company the next day who wanted to talk with us about a possible reality show, and we were excited just to get back to sunny California.

In the past, both Kathy and I have been offered different opportunities from such production companies to work on this type of show. But let's just say that the right idea for us has not come along yet.

As we were getting comfortable and adjusting our seat belts, the announcement came over the PA from the pilot that although we were about to take off, we could experience a little turbulence along the way, due to the inclement weather. Of course, it's not unusual to feel some bumps every now and then as you fly across the sky, but we just hoped it wasn't going to be too bumpy. Neither Kathy nor I have any fear of flying, but we can get hit with motion sickness if the choppy ride becomes a problem.

So, as we took off and headed straight into the sky, the bumps and some slight jolts did rattle the plane for a bit, but the overcast sky became lighter and lighter until we broke through the gray clouds where the sun and blue sky gave us a welcome sight. We then leveled off and the flight became smooth as it began our journey west.

As we settled in and Kathy and I were discussing what the possible snacks were on this trip (something of course very important if you are a flyer, LOL) a woman who was sitting in front of us turned to peek around the seat, then began speaking to us.

"Are you Patrick and Kathy?" the woman asked.

Taking a moment to see if I recognized who she was, which I didn't, I answered her question. "Yes."

"I thought so!" she replied, smiling. "Sorry to bother you, but I just wanted you to know that I am a big fan!"

"Oh, that's so nice of you," Kathy replied, and I agreed. "What is your name?" I asked.

Excitedly she replied, "Marta."

"Like *The Sound of Music* Marta?" I asked. (Yes, I'm a big fan of the movie.)

"Yes, that's right!" she said.

Both Kathy and I responded, saying it was nice to meet her.

She continued, "I've read all your books and they have helped me so much since I lost my son Blake."

"Ohhh, we're so sorry to hear that," I said. Kathy agreed.

"Thank you," Marta responded, "I miss him every day." Tears started to form in her eyes.

"You know your wonderful son Blake is always with you," Kathy consoled her.

"I know, I know. I just wish he was still here," Marta said.

With that, all of a sudden, I saw the figure of a young man standing behind this woman. It's not hard for me to put two and two together to know that more than likely this was Blake who showed up right on cue.

Again, it's not uncommon from time to time that I will sense spirits with people when I am not "working," but I usually will not say anything because it may not be the right time or place. I also never know how a person is going to respond if I just go up to them and tell them a "dead" person has something to say to them! Believe me, I've had it happen and sometimes they're very happy with the encounter; other times I get some very strange looks.

But in this case, with Marta's knowing who we were, I was sure it would be okay.

"Would you be surprised if I told you your son is with you right now?" I asked Marta.

With a surprised look in her eyes, she replied loudly, "He is?" Tears began to stream from Marta's eyes.

"Yes, I see him right now standing behind you," I said.

She turned around to see if she too could see him and then turned back to us.

"Is he still here? I don't see him," she asked anxiously, continuing to speak at a high volume.

Smiling, Kathy then placed her finger to lips to signal to Marta to speak softer so as not to cause a commotion.

I responded in a whisper, "Yes, he is still here. Give me one second and let's see what he has to say." As Marta looked over the seat anxiously, waiting, I took a moment to make a connection with her son.

"Blake first and foremost wants you to know how proud he is of you and your family," I said.

More tears started to fall from her eyes. Kathy took some tissue out of her purse and handed it to her.

I continued, "He is showing me a flag. Was he in the service?"

"Oh my gosh, yes, he was! We were so very proud of him. I mean, we 'are' so proud of him. I know that you said we need to refer to our passed loved ones as if they are in the present tense," she said excitedly.

Kathy responded, "That's right, because they *are* in the present tense!"

"Well I can tell you that he is happy his mom knows that. He's smiling and using his hand to make a mouth motion, mocking you, as if you talk a lot!"

"I do! I do!" she said as she started to get loud again. "He always told me that I talk too much, but I knew he was only kidding me."

"And he still is kidding you," I said with a smile. I continued to listen to Blake.

"Your son is saying to me that you have seen him," I said.

She thought hard for a moment and replied, "I'm not sure. There was one time when I got out of bed and I thought I saw someone in the hall. It scared me to death! But my eyes adjusted and there was actually no one there."

As she was telling us her experience, her son was shaking his head yes.

"Well that was him; you did see him!" I said.

"It was?" she asked.

"Yes, when you are in that 'sleepy mode,' your sixth sense becomes stronger. When you walked into the hall, he was standing there, and you did in fact see him. But once you became fully awake, your vision ended. It is the same now, as I see him and you are unable to," I said.

She replied, "I am so happy to hear that!"

"He says that you also take too long in the bathroom," I added.

She screamed, "He always told me that!"

Kathy placed her finger to her lips again to soften Marta's voice and said in a whisper, "See, you are still making him wait!" We all laughed.

"I do feel him with me all the time and I know he is watching over me," Marta said.

"Blake is telling me you know he is and in fact, he was even holding your hand during the turbulence."

"I was talking with him at that time!" she said loudly. And then in a whisper she said, "Oh, I'm sorry... I need to keep my voice down!" Kathy and I smiled.

"Well he wants you to know that he does hear every word you and your family say to him and to know that he is always going to be keeping an eye out for all of you. He is also saying 'brother' and is showing me a cake. Does he have a brother?"

"Yes, he does! His younger brother is Carl and his birthday is coming up!"

"Well make sure to wish him a happy birthday from his older brother."

"That is going to make Carl so happy!" she exclaimed.

"Fantastic," I replied. "Well again, he is giving everyone his love. And make sure you continue to be the example to everyone how to keep your continuing connection with him going!"

"I will, I will!" Marta again said loudly. Trying to whisper again, she continued, "Thank you so much, the both of you. This was such a surprise and I cannot express how much it has meant to me."

"That's so sweet to hear," Kathy said. "Now you do as your son is telling you and keep those connections strong!"

I smiled and said, "You'd better, or Blake just might lock you out of your bathroom!" We all laughed.

Marta sat back into her seat as a flight attendant started to come around and began delivering the snacks. I could see through the seats Marta clapping her hands together with excitement for what had just taken place and that put a great big smile on both Kathy's face and mine. That, along with the snack being ice cream … just what we wanted!

24. Horse Sense

Besides the loss of a loved one when it's such a close family member or friend, another loss that can be heartbreaking is that of another type of family member, a pet. And if you are a pet owner and have ever experienced this sort of loss, you know exactly what I mean.

Our pets can be as close as our human family, and in many cases, even closer. We give our time and love to our pets, and in return we receive all the joy and unconditional love they can give back. So, it's completely understandable why, when someone has a pet pass into spirit, they can grieve just as hard as if it had been a human being.

When I am giving readings, people will hesitantly at times ask me if I am able to communicate with their beloved pet. Sometimes they seem to be almost embarrassed asking me this as if there would be something wrong with wanting to make a connection with a pet in spirit, or if I am even able to make that connection. But I can.

When I am connecting with an animal in spirit, they will communicate with me telepathically the same as they do with each other here. Although they do not actually speak to me in words, they will give me visual thoughts to relay their messages as well as convey their feelings toward their owner, usually those of love, gratitude, and happiness. From this, I am able to form a message that I will then relay to their owner.

There will also be times for that person when a loved one in spirit will need to be the one that relays a message from a pet, as sometimes the pet will be too excited to do that, running around between me and their owner, thereby not able to make a connection with me.

Hey, pets in spirit get excited too!

Speaking of excited, I recall once speaking with a woman named Rita. Rita came to me in hopes of learning if she had made the right decision.

I explained to Rita how the reading would proceed and then I began.

"Okay Rita, who would you like me to connect with today?" I asked.

"Patrick. I know that my loved ones in spirit are with me and I speak with them all the time. But would they be angry if I wanted to speak with someone else?" Rita asked.

"Of course not!" I responded. "Your loved ones know you love them and I assure you by speaking to them, you make them happy all the time. So, I promise you they will not be angry if you would like for me to connect with another person. What is the relationship of this individual?"

There was silence for a moment as Rita took a few seconds before hesitantly answering.

"Could you speak to my horse for me?" Rita asked sheepishly.

Okay, that took me by surprise, I thought to myself! Usually when a person wants me to connect with a beloved pet, it's a cat or dog. And although I have made connections with other types of animals, asking me to connect with a horse was not an everyday occurrence. But hey, for Rita, I was happy to give it a try.

"Well I will certainly do my best for you, Rita. Give me a moment or two while I open myself up and let me see if I can make this connection for you," I said.

"Thank you so much, Patrick," Rita responded.

I took a moment, closed my eyes and waited to see what was about to transpire. Just as with every reading I give, I will open myself up to the connections between this world and the spirit world and wait to see who will meet me in between. As I started to sense a spirit coming to me, I noticed not only a woman starting to connect, but she was also pulling a horse alongside her.

I said, "Rita, I have a woman coming through to me and she does in fact have your horse with her."

"I'm so excited!" Rita exclaimed.

"This woman is coming to me as a grandmother would, is your mother's mother in spirit?" I asked.

"She is!" Rita said. "I knew Nana would be with Ginger, I just knew it!"

I took a moment and concentrated to see what Rita's grandmother had to say.

I continued. "Well Nana is smiling and wants you to know that she of course is with Ginger. She says that Ginger made it over just fine!"

Rita began to cry. "I hope so," she said, fighting through her tears.

Right then, I not only felt the nurturing love coming from Rita's grandmother, but also from her horse as well.

"Rita, Ginger is now connecting to me and let me tell you, this horse loves you very much!" I said.

"I love her so much; she meant the world to me," Rita said, as she continued to weep.

"She knows this and knows how much you love her. Keep in mind, just like with your grandmother, when you think about Ginger, she receives every thought, as well as your continuing love for her," I said.

This made Rita smile through her tears.

I continued. "Ginger is now showing me a brush."

"Yes, yes, I used to brush her all the time. She was my big baby," Rita said. "I miss brushing her."

Again, I felt so much love coming from Ginger and relayed it to Rita.

"Rita, your horse is now giving me a sadness about you from a decision you had to make. Did you have to put her to sleep?"

With that, Rita broke down into tears, and in a broken voice, answered, "I did. She got a virus and became very ill." Rita couldn't continue.

"I'm so sorry about that, Rita," I said.

I could see Rita's grandmother stand behind her and give her a big hug. She began to speak to me and I took a moment to listen.

"Rita, your grandmother is standing behind you now and giving you a big hug. She is telling me you should stop this foolishness and know that you had no choice. You did not want Ginger to suffer any more," I told her.

"I was praying for her to let me know if I had to do this. Patrick, it was the hardest decision I had to make in my life," Rita said.

"Well your grandmother wants you to know that it was the right thing to do and at the right time," I said. "She knows how hard it was for you and that she was helping you every step of the way."

"I did feel Nana with me," Rita replied.

"She also wants me to tell you that it was no one's fault the way Ginger got the virus, it was just an act of nature," I said.

Rita said, "I know, I know. I keep telling myself that."

"Rita, you are hearing your grandmother telling you that as well," I said. "She's telling me you have her stubbornness, among many other fine attributes of hers."

"I know that is right," Rita said, with a slight smile on her face.

With that, I could sense Ginger wanting to chime in with the conversation. Yes, animals in spirit can get impatient too ...

"Rita, Ginger is connecting with me again and showing me a pony."

"I just got a foal!" Rita said excitedly. "I was wondering if she knew."

I said, "Of course, she knows. I'm sure she even helped you to get it."

"Funny you said that, Patrick," Rita replied.

"Why's that?" I asked.

"Because a few days after Ginger's passing, I of course was still overwhelmed with grief. I was crying at home when the phone rang from a neighbor. He called to tell me that his horse just gave birth and that the person who wanted the foal had to back out and asked if I could take it. I told him I had to think about it and would let him know. So, the next day or two as I was pondering it, I felt such a positive feeling about getting the foal that I told my neighbor I would be happy to take him."

With that, I felt such love from both Nana and Ginger.

"Well I can guarantee, from the positive feelings I am receiving from both your grandmother and Ginger, you made the right choice!"

At that moment, something unusual occurred. I received an image of a grocery store from Ginger. I thought that was strange coming from a horse and had no idea what it meant. But like always, I just went with the flow and hoped it would make some kind of sense.

I continued, "I know this sounds strange, but is there a reason I need to bring up a grocery store to you? Ginger is showing me a grocery store, for some reason!"

"Oh my god!" Rita shouted. "I can't believe this!"

"What?" I asked.

"I was just at the grocery store yesterday and I felt Ginger with me! I thought I was crazy going down the aisles thinking she was actually with me, but I really felt her there!"

"Well see, you are not crazy!" I said. "This is a wonderful confirmation that you yourself connect with Ginger as well!

"That's wonderful! But why would Ginger be in a grocery store with me?" Rita asked.

I responded, "Let me ask you a question first. I assume that you may have felt Ginger before, perhaps in a barn or in a field, yes?"

"Yes, I have."

"And I bet when this happens, you just chalk it up to strong memories or wishful thinking…"

"I do that!" Rita answered.

"Well see, this was a way for Ginger to let you know that the connection you feel with her is not just your imagination. When you are in a location that you shared with someone in spirit, it is not uncommon to actually sense that spirit with you. But many will push this off as just wishful thinking on their part, when it is an actual connection taking place.

"There would be no reason for you to sense Ginger in a store with you, but you did. And by hearing this confirmation, it's for you to understand that you do in fact connect with her! I'm sure she is even the one that helped you by giving you the positive feeling about getting the foal!"

"I see!" Rita said happily. "I understand now that she is really with me." This made her smile.

Rita then asked, "Is Ginger healthy now?"

Of course I knew she was and was about to say so, when I saw Rita's grandmother laughing, knowing what I was about to say …

"Rita, I promise … Ginger is healthy as a horse!"

Rita also laughed, now assured that her big baby will always be with her. I think I also saw Ginger smiling as well.

25. Removing the Fear

One thing is true about being a medium: through the countless readings I have given, not only have I learned much about Heaven and the afterlife, but I've also learned about people. I have experienced people when they have been at their very lowest in life as well as those who are their most joyful. And with each reading I give, I will usually learn something I may not have known before and will collectively use this knowledge in helping many others, no matter where they are on the emotional spectrum. Every reading adds a new perspective to life and the afterlife.

For many varied reasons, people come to me hoping I am able to connect with their loved ones in spirit. My readings range from those who are deeply grieving, in desperate need to hear from a dear relative, to others who just want to say hi and catch up with an old friend. Everyone has their reasons.

And no matter the reason for the reading, I treat each and every reading I give with the upmost respect and compassion it deserves. When I am giving a reading, there is a certain amount of pressure I place on myself, as I want the experience to be as wonderful for the person receiving it as it is to me. But there is one situation where I place more pressure on myself than any other, and this is when I am giving a reading to someone who is terminally ill.

We all have, located somewhere way in the back of our minds, the knowledge that we're going to pass into spirit one day...but that's "one day." And we tend to think that one day is not going to be tomorrow, nor next week, probably not even next year. That one day is sometime way off in the far-distant future when we are very old and have lived a long, long life.

But unfortunately, every day, people receive the negative news that they have a terminal illness. From that moment on, they know there's not going to be a next year, and for some, not even a next month. And even if the person receiving this news is the bravest of all, their life from then on will never be the same. They know that the end of their life is now approaching and that "one day" is now "soon."

It is devastating for people who receive such news. Even those with the strongest beliefs in God and an afterlife can still be afraid of the journey they are about to embark on, not knowing for sure what they are going to go through physically, but more important, what actually will happen to them after they depart this realm.

So, when someone who is terminally ill comes to me for a reading, I have only one goal in mind, and that is to do my best to remove any fear they may be experiencing by helping them to not only *believe*, but to *know* there really is an afterlife.

I recall once speaking with a woman named Jennifer who had been diagnosed with terminal cancer. Her friend Allison, whom I had spoken to in the past, set up an appointment for her to speak with me over the phone. As I began speaking with Jennifer, I could hear by the quiver in her voice that she was afraid. So, with this, I told her just to take a few deep breaths and tell me what she feared.

"I'm afraid of dying," Jennifer replied, crying.

"I know, I know," I said, my heart going out to her. "I am so sorry to hear about your situation."

At that moment, before I even had a chance to ask what spirits she would like me to connect with, I felt several of her relatives starting to reach out to me.

I continued. "I can tell you right now that you not only have your dear friend Susanne's support, but there are several spirits coming to me all at once who are very anxious to speak with you."

"I so need to hear from them," Jennifer replied through tears.

I took a moment, made my connections with the spirits around me, and proceeded.

"Your father and mother are here and they both are trying to talk over each other," I said.

This made Jennifer giggle. "That sure sounds like them," she replied.

"Well tell them to behave themselves, because I can only concentrate when listening to one of them at a time!" I replied.

This made Jennifer laugh. "Behave yourselves, Mom and Dad!" Jennifer said loudly.

"Okay, I think they listened, as I can tell you your mother is now going to be the one talking first," I said.

"I thought she would win out," Jennifer replied.

I took a moment and concentrated on Jennifer's mother's message. "First, your mother wants to tell you that both she and your father know what you are going through. I can also tell you, I am feeling so much love and compassion from them for you."

Jennifer began to cry, making me tear up as well.

"Your mother is also telling me that you and both of your parents were and are extremely close," I said.

"I love both of them so very much," Jennifer replied.

"Well they continue to feel your love and I know that you have been feeling theirs, especially during this time in your life," I said.

"I have, very strongly," Jennifer confirmed.

"Your father is shouting at me the name Lin or Linda," I said.

Jennifer exclaimed, "That's my mother's name!"

"Well I don't know if he's shouting at her or at me to give you that confirmation!" I said, laughing.

Jennifer answered, "No, that's Dad, he just always had a booming voice!"

"He is telling me he had to, living with you and your mother!" I said. Jennifer continued laughing.

"Okay, I guess I'm with your dad now," I told Jennifer. With that, I took a moment to listen to what Jennifer's father had to say.

"Your dad is telling me that both he and your mother are so very proud of you. He says they've always been, but especially now with what you are experiencing," I told Jennifer.

She said, "Yes, they always told me how proud they were of me."

"By the way, I said what 'you' were experiencing, but your father is correcting me and wants me to say what you *all* are going through, as you know they are going through it with you!"

"I have felt them with me. They were such strong people here and I am trying to be just as strong," she affirmed.

"They *are* strong people," I told her, "and your dad is saying for you to lay your troubles on his shoulders."

"Oh my gosh," she exclaimed. "He would always say that whenever I had worries or problems!"

"He's telling me that you are his baby girl and always will be," I assured her.

I now started to hear Jennifer's mother speaking, so I then had to concentrate on her.

"Jennifer, your mother wants to speak. Although I usually will spend some time with one spirit and then perhaps another, your parents have me going back and forth, back and forth."

"Welcome to my world!" Jennifer said, laughing.

This statement made everyone chuckle.

"Your mother is telling me they heard that!" I said, laughing.

"Uh oh!" Jennifer replied.

"I sense your mother's feelings are changing right now. She and your father as well are letting me feel such compassion and the strong love they have for you with what she wants to say. Your mother wants you to know that even though you have been putting on a brave face for everyone, they know what is going on inside you. They want you to know it's natural to be afraid, they too also felt the same way when it was their time to pass into spirit."

With that, I heard Jennifer's father begin to speak up.

"Wait one second, Jennifer, your dad now wants to add on to that. Your father is telling me that he was not at all afraid of his passing."

And with that, I asked him to let me feel what had happened to him and I had a burst of pain in my chest area.

"Jennifer, did your father pass from a heart attack?" I asked.

"Yes, he did! He was out playing tennis with some friends. They said he was playing fine and then he just dropped. It happened that fast," she told me.

"Well no wonder he wasn't afraid, he didn't have time to be!" I said, adding my own two cents.

This made everyone laugh, while Jennifer's father stood there just shaking his head.

I continued, "Going back to what your mother was saying. She is giving me the feeling that she passed from cancer."

Jennifer said, "She did."

"She is showing me that you were with her," I added.

"I was with her the whole time," Jennifer replied.

"And she is also showing me you standing close to her, but this was not always the case."

Softly, Jennifer replied, "We had our ups and downs, but we became very close during her illness."

"Well she wants you to know how much that time between you two meant to her and that your love for her is what helped to take away the fear that she too was experiencing during those days. Your wonderful mother and, of course, your father want you to also know that just like with what you did for your mother, they too are by your side, every minute, taking care of you, in only the ways spirits who love you are able."

This made both Jennifer and myself tear up.

"Keep in mind, what you are going through is just one chapter in your ever-continuing life. Your father is now speaking and is telling me assuredly you are going to be with them, and when that day comes, Heaven for them will be even brighter," I told her.

Hearing this made Jennifer start to cry. And with the love I felt from her parents, along with that message from a father to his little girl, I too became teary-eyed.

Just then, I felt another spirit starting to approach me who wanted to join in on the conversation...

I told her, "Jennifer, someone else is here. Do you also have a brother in spirit? There is a spirit coming to me as a brother would."

"Yes, I can't believe it! His name is John and he passed a long time ago," she exclaimed.

"Well he's telling me to tell you that the old saying is true, the 'good' do die young, but he doesn't know what your excuse will be."

At hearing that comment, Jennifer and I both laughed out loud, as it was so unexpected.

"Tell him I am going to get him back when I'm finally over there!" Jennifer laughingly replied.

"He says to ask you what makes you think you're even going to make it there? John says that only good people go to Heaven and you don't fit the bill!"

"If that were truly the case, he would not be 'upstairs' himself!"

That remark then made us laugh all over again.

"He says you still know how to keep him in line."

"I always will."

For the rest of the reading, Jennifer seemed to be in a more jovial mood and relaxed while she continued hearing wonderful messages and confirmations from her dear family.

After the reading, Jennifer appeared relieved and told me she was so thankful for the reading with me. I said she was a special soul and that she was going to be helping more people through this experience than she could ever imagine.

A couple of months later, I heard from her friend Allison, and she gave me the news that Jennifer had passed into spirit. Allison told me that ever since Jennifer received her reading, she had been in a happier place, knowing that all her loved ones in spirit were truly with her, helping her every day and that she would be home with them again.

Hearing this placed a smile on my face, and while listening to Allison, Jennifer suddenly came through to me. So of course, I wanted to hear what she had to tell both Allison and myself.

First, Jennifer wanted us to know that she made it over just fine, and that she was with her "crazy" family. She also stated that knowing what she knows now, she would not trade what she had to go through with her illness for the world. She said that she now understood the importance of it and that it not only became a benefit to her, but to others as well. Jennifer also said she did find out that the "end" is really only a beginning, the beginning of a continuous life that is truly unimaginably wonderful.

I could feel the joy exuding from her spirit.

Jennifer also said that she would be keeping an eye on Allison and she would be the one helping her find love in her life. Allison thanked her and told Jennifer she would take all the help she could get!

There is a great responsibility being a medium, especially when comes to situations like this. People who are placed in such a circumstance are naturally and understandably afraid, and my heart goes out to each and every one of them. And if I can help remove even a little fear they may be experiencing, I too will take something away.

26. Old Soul, Young Spirit

I have an "old soul."

And for those of you who also have an old soul, you know exactly what it is I am speaking about.

The term *old soul* describes a feeling, or a knowing, a wisdom in your soul. It is the sense you have inside of maturity, which is hard to explain; it's just an awareness. In actuality, having an old soul means that your soul has reincarnated in many lives, or to put it another way: it's been "around the block" a few times.

But the funny thing is, I also have a "young spirit."

Are the two the same?

No. Let me explain why...

The type of spirit I am referring to as being "young" is not an actual "spirit," but more of the way I perceive life, my "spirit of mind," let's say. It is how I look at life and my attitude toward it.

It's so easy to mentally get bogged down with the everyday challenges that life can bring. And although the challenges of life we go through give our souls an opportunity to learn and to grow, this also can burden one's mindset in how they understand this life.

With the work that I do, every day I experience the sadness and grief that comes from those who want me to connect with their loved ones in spirit. And as mentioned previously, emotion is energy, energy is physical, and energy can be received. Being that I am extremely sensitive to energy, I do receive and experience this energy from people when I am at work.

And when doing so, it can wear on me at times, not only physically, but mentally as well, since I do have a habit of caring too much. But I don't find that to be a fault.

Of course, by the end of any reading I give, I hope that I have lessened any grief a person may have been experiencing, replacing it with a certainty that their loved ones continue to be with them, giving them a new perspective on how they can continue their lives with the ones they love in spirit.

Not only can this change the course of their lives, but also their spirit life as well.

———

I remember speaking with one man named Pete whose wife had passed into spirit. He was a gentle soul and a kind man in his seventies and felt that without his beloved wife, he could not foresee any future. He had no family and being all alone in his house, he would just sit for hours every day thinking about the past. With nothing left to lose, he decided to speak with me.

"I've never done anything like this before," Pete started out, sounding very nervous.

"I haven't either," I said, and waited for a response.

Dead silence followed and then I told him I was just kidding. He laughed and the ice was broken.

I told him, "I promise those nerves are going to disappear in just a moment or two."

"Okay," Pete said. After taking a minute and explaining how I worked, I asked Pete who I could try to connect with and he responded he wanted to speak with his wife Brenda. I waited a moment and reached out to her.

I began, "Okay, Brenda is here and the first thing she is doing is patting her heart, and I do feel an ache in my chest. Did she pass from a heart attack?" I asked.

Pete responded in a surprised but low voice, "She did. It was unexpected."

I said, "Brenda says that it was unexpected for her as well. She is telling me that she did not have or feel any signs beforehand that it was going to take place."

"I wanted to ask her that," Pete replied. "I didn't notice her having any issues and wondered if there was something she had been hiding from me."

I waited for Brenda's response. I said, "Brenda is telling me that you know she would never hide anything from you and that she really had no idea this was going to take place. She also wants you to know that she felt no pain." Pete was relieved to hear this.

I continued, "Pete, Brenda is also giving me the feeling of being out of it. Was she asleep?"

"Yes, it happened in the middle of the night. We went to bed and everything seemed normal until I woke up to find that she had died in the middle of the night," Pete said, with a quiver in his voice.

"I'm so sorry to hear that," I said. "Brenda is giving me so much love and compassion for your having to experience this. But she also wants you to know that there was nothing you could have done about it; it was just her time to be in spirit."

"I still think there might have been something I could have done for her," Pete said.

I replied, "Well Brenda is telling me, that sounds like the stubborn man she loves so much."

Hearing this put a small smile on Pete's face and he replied, "I would do anything for her." With that, I felt Brenda getting excited.

"Brenda says she knows you would do anything for her and there is something important she wants you to do."

"Anything, anything … what is it?" Pete asked.

"Brenda wants you to be happy. She is telling me that you haven't really been living since she has passed. Is this true?" I asked.

"Of course I'm living. I'm just not happy about it," he replied.

"I understand your feelings," I said, "and so does Brenda. But she also knows how much you enjoyed life with her and how important it is for you to continue to do so."

Pete responded, "How can I live without her?"

"That's the key, Pete; it's not without her, as she will be with you every day, loving you as she always has. You just have to understand that even though she is in spirit now, she is still the same beautiful woman, only she is in perfect health and is looking after you, as she always did."

"I want to believe all of this is real, Patrick," Pete said.

With that, I heard Brenda say the word *seashell* and she held a shell up to her head.

"Pete, Brenda is showing me a seashell, is there a connection there with you two?" I asked.

With that, Pete began to sob. After a moment, he gained his composure and responded.

Pete told me, "I was just holding a shell before I called; it was Brenda's. She loved picking up shells when we would go to the beach and we displayed them on the bookshelf."

"Well what a wonderful confirmation to let you know that she is not only alive and well, but is and will always be with you. Brenda is also smiling and saying when you were holding the shell, you were feeling her with you."

"I did," Pete said.

"Well Pete, that's how it works! The more you are open to Brenda being with you, the stronger her presence will be," I explained.

With that, Brenda showed me an image of her and Pete in their house, but she was pushing him out of the house.

"Brenda wants you to get out of your house. She is showing me her pushing you out of the door."

"She would always try to get me to go somewhere," Pete responded.

"Well she still is. It's important for you not to sit there and grow old—her words, not mine—and it's important for you to look forward to your future!"

"But I don't have a future without her."

"Brenda wants you to know first, you do have a future, and second, it is not going to be without her. Just because she is in spirit and understands all the reasons why this has transpired, she also knows and understands your perspective. And so she recognizes what you are going through and this makes her love you more than ever. But she also knows the importance of your moving forward, not alone, but together, as she is and will always be with you."

"I hope she is."

"No hoping, she will be."

At that moment, Brenda showed me a classroom.

"Brenda is showing me you in a school. Do you or did you teach?" I asked.

"No," Pete responded

"Hmm … Brenda keeps showing you in school. Oh, were you thinking about going back to school or taking classes?"

Pete responded, "I was. It's something that I had been thinking about doing before she died. I was interested in sailing and thought it might have been fun taking some courses."

I felt a sense of excitement coming from Brenda. I said, "Well let me tell you, Brenda is extremely happy about the idea. She is telling me that not only should you do it, but she insists that you do."

"The idea pops into my mind every now and then," Pete replied.

Excited, I quickly responded, "And why do you think it just 'pops' into your mind? That's actually Brenda telling you to go do it!"

"I see," Pete said.

I continued, "Brenda wants you to know that she will be with you at these classes, on the boats, and enjoying all that life has to offer. Keep in mind that the more you get out and do things, the less grief you will experience and the stronger your connections with her will become!"

"I can do that," Pete said.

"Good! This makes Brenda very happy!" I said. "She knows what's going on inside your head right now and she is excited for what's ahead, and you should be too," I said.

Pete replied, "She always was excited about the future."

"And some things will never change…" I said.

———

It's important to remember that this "life" we live is just the sum of all the "feelings and emotions" we experience; the "physical" part of this life is really just a springboard to releasing them. Your spirit of mind is something you can control and of course, just like with anything else in life, it's up to you how young it can make you feel.

This is why it is important to have the right mindset when it comes to your life, and a big part of that is looking forward to the future!

You see, in this life, it's important to always look ahead, to have someone or something that will pull you forward. Life is not meant to be lived standing still or stagnant, because doing so will not only stop your spirit from growing, but also your soul.

And although there can be limits to what someone may physically be able to do, there are no limits when it comes to your mind! Many times, just thinking of the possibilities that can be achieved and hoping for a better future can give one the joy and happiness that will forever keep the spirit young!

27. Learning Something New Every Day

One of the greatest things, of many, about being a medium is that I too continue to learn something new from spirits every day. When I am at the start of the reading and begin to make a connection with a spirit for someone, it's like looking at a blank canvas. At the beginning of each reading, I never know where the conversation is going to go, nor how it will end. You can say, just as is true for the person receiving the reading, I too am there along for the ride.

And although when I am giving a reading I may "try" to guide certain aspects of the conversation in one direction, just as in this life when you try to get into a conversation between two people, sometimes you must just let the two go at it, sit back, and experience it.

Specific information in the messages will come through during the reading that confirm to the person receiving it that I am actually speaking with their loved ones in spirit. Each reading is unique in its own way and there can be times when I not only surprise the person hearing from their loved ones in spirit, but I am surprised as well.

Many times, whether in writings, when giving lectures, or in classes, as I give examples about what Heaven is like, of course I personally can't describe it myself as I only have this point of view, so I depend on information straight from the source ... those in spirit!

But the one thing I have learned is that all that I know and all that I share is just a glimpse into what the afterlife is really like.

And why?

It's simple; there are just no words for us in this physical realm to understand the true magnificence of Heaven. But if you know me, that doesn't stop me from trying ...

I recall a phone reading I recently had with a wonderful young woman named Mally.

When I am giving readings by phone, the only thing I will have in front of me is the person's first name, but for some reason, I had misplaced this one and did not have a chance to look at it before the phone rang.

I answered, ready to begin the session.

"Hi, this is Patrick. Before we begin, I want you to know that I usually would have your name right in front of me, but it disappeared on me!"

"Hi Patrick. That's okay, this is Mally," she said.

"Well Molly, nice to be speaking with you today," I responded.

"No, it's Mally. It's Irish," she stated with a laugh, as she corrected me.

"Oh, I see, I thought you were just saying Molly with a strong New England accent!" I said. We both laughed.

I asked her if she had to go through that all the time with her name, and she confirmed that she did. She told me she was more than happy to do so because it was the name of her grandmother, whom she loved so very much. As she was telling me this, I could all of sudden sense her grandmother with me and asked if that was who she wanted to connect with. She said it was and I responded that I was happy it was because she was the one there and was ready to speak! I could instantly feel the love that her grandmother had for Mally. She was strong, protective, and wise.

"Mally," I said, "Your wonderful grandmother is telling me she is so happy that you have her name. She says that you two not only share a name, but you look very much like her."

"I do!" Mally responded. "It seems the older I get, the more and more I resemble her."

"Well being in Heaven, your grandmother is saying that she has knocked a few years off herself, so the younger she gets, the more she is looking like you!" I told her.

We all laughed at that one, as it seemed Mally's grandmother had a wonderful sense of humor.

"Mally, your grandmother is letting you know that she has been keeping an eye out for you," I said.

"Well that could be trouble," she said, laughing.

"Now you've made your grandmother laugh," I said. "Your grandmother is showing me a ring."

With that, Mally let out a small yelp and explained in excitement, "I just became engaged!"

"Well your grandmother is excited too and congratulating you! From me, too, of course. And she wants you to know that she cannot wait to see you walk down the aisle!" I said.

After a few seconds, I could hear Mally begin to cry.

"Oh my gosh, I was just saying to my mother that I wished Gran could be here to see me and be with me on this special day," Mally said.

I replied, "Well now you know she will be there, in the front row, no less, as that is what she is telling me."

We all laughed.

Then Mally asked me, "I picked a special day for the wedding. Is she aware of that?"

"Let me ask," I replied.

After a moment, Mally's grandmother held up a cake, usually signifying to me that a spirit is indicating a birthday or an anniversary.

"Does the date have anything to do with a birthday or anniversary?" I asked.

"It does!" Mally shouted. "I thought it would be wonderful to get married on her birthday! I always wanted a May wedding and this date would work out perfectly for us as Gran's birthday was in May!"

With that I could feel a sense of not only joy, but pride coming from Mally's grandmother.

"I can tell you that your grandmother could not be happier," I told her.

Mally was extremely pleased to hear this!

She replied, "I was hoping to hear that! When I was in the beginning planning stages of my wedding, it just popped into my head and it felt so right!"

"Well guess who put that idea into your head? It was your grandmother, that's who!" I replied. "This is how connection with a loved one in spirit works! And that feeling you had was you sensing your grandmother's happiness," I said.

"I see!" Mally replied. "I hope that she is going to help me with the rest of my wedding planning."

Mally's grandmother was all joy at hearing this, and responded, "She is telling me that nothing would bring her more happiness."

This brought tears of joy to Mally.

I continued, "But make sure to get your mother's advice as well, as she is excited too," her grandmother relayed to me.

"Oh, I will!" Mally responded with a laugh.

A few more topics came up in discussion, with more advice given by Mally's grandmother, when Mally asked a question I often hear.

"Patrick, my grandmother was a firm believer in Heaven. Sometimes we would talk about what Heaven is really like. Could you ask her to tell me what it is like for her?"

As long as I have been a medium, I have known that there are no real words with which a spirit can convey, explain, or describe exactly all that Heaven is and what being in spirit is really like, but I always invite them to give it a try. I find it's interesting to see what those in spirit can come up with, and Mally's grandmother decided to give it a try.

"Mally, first your grandmother is saying being in Heaven and in spirit is better than anything you have experienced here or could ever discuss. She says the beauty of Heaven is something unimaginable and as much as she wishes she could put it into words, she is unable. And here is an example why..."

I continued.

"Right now, Mally, your grandmother is asking you to pretend you are a preschooler. You are sitting at a desk and she is in front of you holding up the different letters of the alphabet. She shows you the letter A then B and so forth until all the letters are shown. It takes you time, but you slowly start to learn each of them.

"Now let's say all of a sudden, she is placing a dictionary in front of you. You open it and although you can see all the letters you just learned, you have no idea nor are you able to understand all the countless words that are in that book. The only thing you are able to grasp are the individual letters.

She is telling me that this is the same for her when describing Heaven. In this life, we are only learning the alphabet and those in spirit are fluent in the dictionary."

When I heard this, I thought to myself how cool an answer that was, and I responded.

"Mally, I never heard it put that way before, the way she said that. I think I will use her example in a book of mine sometime!"

We all laughed, and Mally responded, "I like it too. It makes it easier to understand that it's just one of those things that you have to experience yourself in order to know fully what it is like."

"And your grandmother is saying with a smile, that goes for marriage too…"

We all laughed.

So, as you can see, it's not just the person who is receiving a reading who is learning something; I too can find a new understanding as well. I know that I am only scratching the surface as to what Heaven and the afterlife really are, but that's okay; that's what makes my job or any other job interesting. In other words, I'm learning something new every day.

28. Sweet Tooth Spirit

I enjoy a good doughnut just like everyone else, and from time to time, if I spot a new bakery on my travels, I will stop in to see what new and exciting pastries they have to offer.

I recall once going into a small but quaint shop, not very big at all. But let me tell you, not only were the display cases filled with beautiful and mouthwatering pastries and doughnuts, but the smells from the stunning desserts filled the shop, so much so that it "made you want to slap your Mama!" (Kathy and I were in the UK once and she used that term with some people we were with from there. They laughed at us like we were both crazy, but by the end of our trip, they were all saying it! I guess it's just a Southern expression ...)

There were doughnuts of every kind: Boston cream, lemon, sour cream, plus bear claws, apple fritters, and a variety of cookies, cakes, and pies. Anyway, as I stood there and perused the enticing assortment, I noticed the woman behind the counter staring at me as she waited on the customer that was before me.

As I kept my eyes on the doughnuts, looking over the selections and deciding what I would like to purchase, I could also sense the presence of a spirit walking around. *Okay*, I thought, *I'm sure spirits like a good donut every now and then and that's probably why they are making their presence known to me.* But who was I kidding, I know the difference between a spirit just being around me and when one actually wants to communicate. This spirit wanted to communicate.

While this was taking place, the customer before me paid for his purchase and left, and the woman behind the counter came up to me. Reading Vicky on her nametag, I greeted her and asked how she was doing. She replied that she was doing fine and inquisitively looked at me, saying that I looked familiar. I know when I hear the words, "I look familiar," one of two things is about to occur…

One, they know I'm "that guy who speaks to dead people." Or two, they think I'm the actor from the Harry Potter movies, Alan Rickman. (Alan Rickman passed away a while ago … but somehow, people from time to time still think I am him, or at least look like him.)

So, when someone tells me I look familiar, I know that it will probably be one of the two, so deciding to cut to the chase and combining the two, I said to Vicky, "I am the guy from the Harry Potter movies who talks with dead people."

Vicky laughed and told me she thought I was Patrick Mathews and that she was a big fan. She said she had read all my books and was excited that I was in her shop. I smiled and thanked her for her kind words and said I was happy to hear that she enjoyed my books. But as soon as she proceeded to ask what kind of donuts I would like, the spirit who I noticed earlier was ready to give his order. But it was not for donuts; he wanted me to give a message to Vicky.

Though it appeared as if I was focusing on the selection of doughnuts, I was actually beginning to concentrate more on what this spirit wanted to say to Vicky. First, I could tell that the man was Vicky's father. I can identify this by a certain energy a spirit has. Quickly opening myself up more in order to connect with this spirit better, I asked him what he would like to tell her.

While I began listening to this spirit, Vicky looked at me, noticing that I was now paying attention to something or someone else. She became excited, asking me if I was talking with a spirit. Of course, at this point, I knew that it was okay to let her know that I was, and I asked if her father was in spirit. With that question, her eyes began to well up and with her lips quivering, she replied yes. I smiled and told her that her father was here, and asked if it was okay for me to give her a message from him. She responded that she would love it.

I then concentrated on Vicky's father, who also seemed just as excited for this opportunity. He began by telling Vicky that he was always with her and was proud of what she had done with the shop. Vicky responded that it was her father's bakery to begin with and she took it over after his passing. This pleased him very much.

He then told me that he wanted her to know that he was happy she had found love in her life and that her boyfriend better be good to her or else he would have to deal with him. She laughed and relayed that she had found the one and had wondered what her dad would think of him. She told her father that she would be sure to give her boyfriend that message!

Her father then showed me a cake. When I am shown this image from a spirit, it usually means there is a birthday or anniversary taking place soon and the spirit wants that person to know they are aware of this taking place. But seeing this, I just thought her father was again referring back to all of us being in their bakery. When I told Vicky what her father was showing me, she broke down and cried, smiling at the same time. She then ran into the back of the store and brought out a cake.

On top of the cake were written the words "Happy Birthday, Dad!"

Vicky explained it happened to be her father's birthday that day and she decided to make him a special cake. While doing so, she thought she felt her father with her and hoped he would give her some sign that he was with her. She told me that when I walked into her shop, she knew that she had received her sign.

I smiled and told Vicky that I was happy to have been her sign and knew her father loved her very much and appreciated the cake. Her father said that although it would not disappear from the plate physically, he actually would eat the whole thing ... or he may even share it with others in spirit.

This brought a big smile to Vicky's face and she said for me to tell her father how much she loved him. I told her that he just heard her say those words and that she also just put a great big smile on his face.

With that, a bell hanging on the door rang, signifying another customer was coming into the shop. We both smiled at each other and I went on to place my order. Vicky was nice enough to offer it for free, and although I told her how kind that was of her, I said she didn't have to do that. But she insisted.

I was happy that Vicky continued to celebrate her father's birthday. And if the donuts were any sign of her baking skills, I know that her father and others in spirit also enjoyed the birthday cake!

PART 5
LAST WORDS

I would now like to share with you a few more thoughts, touching experiences, and some humorous encounters I have had.

Also, as you can imagine, I am often asked many questions about my work, spirits, and the afterlife, and hope that the following questions and answers I have included will help to answer some of yours.

29. In Touch Questions and Answers

It goes without saying that I receive many questions about the afterlife and the work that I do. People want to know anything from what life is like for those on the Other Side to what life is like for me as someone who is able to communicate one on one with spirits. Not only do the answers to these questions come from what I have learned from those in spirit, but also with my own personal experiences living the life that I do. So, I hope that the following questions and answers can help shed some light on things that you too were wondering.

Do I See Spirits All the Time?

A lot of people think that just because I can communicate with those in spirit must mean that I see them all around, all the time.

This is not true.

When I am "Medium Patrick Mathews" and I am going to connect with a spirit for someone, I need to take a moment and focus on what I am about to do. I clear my mind and open my sixth sense up, so that the spirit I will be communicating with will come to me, making the connection, and then I will relay the messages they wish to convey to their loved one I am speaking to. When I am done, I will then do the opposite and shut off my sixth sense, thereby ending the communication with spirits.

But—and you knew there would be a but—when I am out and about, I will every now and then sense or see spirits around me without opening myself up to them. Keep in mind that spirits, being people, all have their own personalities just like us, but part of their personality also consists of how strong an energy they have. So sometimes when I am out in public I can't help but connect with them, the same way as if you were to put two magnets close to each other and they would connect. And that connection can also happen when I least expect it if a spirit pushes themselves on me to make a connection.

If I do go outside being "on," yes, I will sense or see spirits all around as they of course continue to be with their loved ones here.

HOW OLD WAS I
WHEN I FIRST SAW A SPIRIT?

Although I was told that when I was a toddler I would speak out loud to people who were not there (or let's just say, they couldn't be seen), my actual recollection of my first communication with a spirit was when I was six years old.

I was in bed one night and I was awakened by a man standing near my bed, that being an uncle who had recently passed. I knew it was not an actual person standing there, as he appeared somewhat transparent and I was able to hear him speak to me in my head. He wanted me to assure everyone in the family that he was safe, in perfect health, and that he would be watching over the family. Yes, I was very scared at first, but the feeling of love that came from him did calm me down.

Do I communicate with my family in spirit?

I would have to say this is one of the greatest benefits of having this gift, being able to continue to communicate with my loved ones in spirit.

I feel very fortunate to have the ability to keep in touch with my family in spirit, and just like those I give readings to, I too ask my loved ones for guidance in my life. Do I get all the answers I want? Nope! I've been communicating with spirits long enough to know that there are things they are allowed to say or to help with and other things they cannot.

Keep in mind: although I have the ability of communicating with spirits stronger than most, the other greatest part of my gift is in helping others to understand and to recognize their own communications with their family in spirit!

What is the difference between connecting with a spirit and receiving a sign from a spirit?

A sign from a spirit is when they make their presence known by manipulating or maneuvering a physical item or object.

A connection with a spirit is when they will actually communicate with a person, and that person receives a message through one of their five (or six) senses.

Can anyone connect with spirts?

Yes!

Everyone actually does connect with their loved ones in spirit, pretty much on a daily basis, but this connection will usually take place subconsciously. The good news, however, is that the more a person is aware of the slight nuances of connections, the more conscious or more noticeable the connection can become!

Does everyone receive signs?

Yes!

Everyone can receive signs from their loved ones in spirit. And even though I have listed many in this book to look for, it only scratches the surface. The important thing is, again, just don't ask for a "sign," but ask for something specific, so you know what you should be watching for. Then, after you ask, pay attention to your surroundings for the next week or so, as you never know what you might receive!

DO SPIRITS BECOME BOTHERED BY YOUR COMMUNICATING WITH THEM?

Not at all!

Your loved ones in spirit are and will continue to be with you whether you are aware of them or not. When you talk with them (out loud or to yourself, they hear you either way), this always brings a smile to their faces as they know that you know they are with you. Also, having a conversation with them will set you in the right mindset to actually hear them respond back to you! So chat away!

CAN SOMEONE SPEAK TOO MUCH WITH A SPIRIT?

No, unless this communication hinders that person's life in some way.

It's important to live this life to the fullest, and that includes after the passing of a loved one. And if someone were to stay home all day and just relive memories and speak to their loved ones in spirit, that is not moving forward, that is standing still.

That is why it is so important to move forward in life, along with your loved ones in spirit, living life to its fullest. And by doing so, you can talk your spirit loved one's ear off!

DOES EVERYONE IN THIS WORLD HAVE SPIRITS WITH THEM?

Yes.

From the moment a person is born into this world until the day they pass into spirit, a person will have spirits who will be there for guidance and support throughout their entire life.

WHO ARE THESE SPIRITS?

It really depends on each individual, but they are usually relatives and guides.

When you are born, chances are both parents will still be in this physical realm so it could be a grandparent or even a great-grandparent who is with you in spirit. There can also be aunts and uncles who will participate in your life as well. And as you grow older, these spirits who have been with you will usually take a back seat once a parent or even a spouse should pass into spirit.

There are also what are known as "spirit guides." These are individuals who are not necessarily related to you, but are connected to you by a personality trait, a skill, or any gift you may possess and/or share with them.

And without a doubt, there are angels who are also looking over the whole bunch of us, guiding and loving everyone!

DO SPIRITS GET SOMETHING FOR HELPING US?

Sure they do.

First, keep in mind, it is not a "job" for a loved one in spirit to look after you. They do it from a place of emotion, that being love. Helping and guiding you is giving that spirit a chance to love and protect you; this is causing their soul continuous growth.

DO SPIRITS GET OFFENDED IF I
WOULD PREFER TO HAVE A PARTICULAR
LOVED ONE WATCH OVER ME
RATHER THAN ANOTHER?

Of course your loved ones in spirits do not get offended.

It's natural in this life to be closer to certain people than others, and that includes relatives. Let's say, for example, someone had been extremely close with their parents and wanted them to watch over them, and then their spouse passes. It's only natural for that person now to want that spouse to be the main one with them and the parents certainly will understand this, while continuing to participate as well!

But remember, there is no specific number of how many spirits will be guiding you, just as there are no limits to love.

WHAT IF A PERSON DOES NOT WANT A
CERTAIN SPIRIT TO BE WITH THEM AT ALL?
WILL THEY STAY AWAY?

Each circumstance is different, but you do have some control over who will be participating in your life spiritually.

If you are emotionally connected to someone in spirit, they of course will be the one who will be guiding you in this life. But if a relative that you did not like or you even harbor ill feelings toward is in spirit, chances are they are not going to be the one who will "personally" be guiding you.

Keep in mind, though, whatever the reason for the rift being created, that person in spirit not only understands and is regretful for it, but you should try to feel the same way. Once in spirit, both sides of a situation are clear and that makes understanding it easier.

But this does not mean they are not a part of your life at all; well, at least in a "knowing what's going on with you" kind of way, as I can assure you they would truly be sorry if the fault was on their end and hope that one day you too will feel the same way.

CAN A PERSON MAKE UP WITH A SPIRIT?

By all means, yes!

Remember, it is never too late to make up with someone in spirit.

Many times, during a reading, I hear from people who want me to ask someone in spirit to forgive them. But the fact of the matter is they have already been forgiven. The moment someone decides to ask a being in spirit for forgiveness is the very moment when they are forgiven.

Believe me, spirits rarely hold grudges against those here in this physical world and if someone is at a point of asking for forgiveness, there is spiritual growth for that person wanting to receive this from a spirit.

So never worry if you think you will have to wait until you too are in spirit one day to reconcile any differences you may have with another in spirit. If you are thinking it, you already have done it! So, continue living life, knowing they're living it with you ...

WHAT IF A PERSON DOESN'T WANT ANY SPIRITS TO BE WITH THEM?

So sad, too bad, but everyone is going to have spirits with them in this life, like it or not!

It's the same as if a child wants to go play outside by themselves, and even though the parents let them, they will continue to watch over that child without their knowledge. This is why there is a thin veil between this world and the next, so those in spirit can and will continue to watch over the ones they love here.

IF SOMEONE DOESN'T BELIEVE IN SPIRITS OR AN AFTERLIFE, ARE SPIRITS WITH THEM TOO?

Of course they are! (Not that it matters to that individual anyway ...)

The purpose of the life we live here in the physical realm is really twofold. Not only do we get something from it, but so do those in spirit.

We are given the opportunity to learn and grow (psychologically and/or spiritually) every day by living this life. Those who help us in spirit also have soul growth by giving us their love and care.

Even though an individual does not believe in an afterlife, this does not mean that a loved one in spirit will not still be watching over them. Again, keep in mind that much of the time, guidance from a spirit goes unnoticed, so this would not affect a nonbeliever anyway.

So, does a person have to believe in God, spirits, or an afterlife in order for their soul to grow?

No, they do not.

Soul growth does not come from a person's faith, but instead comes from a person's heart and their actions toward others. Someone could be the most religious person in the world, but if they are not kind, loving, and thankful in life, without these attributes, there is not a lot of soul growth taking place. Also, if they are "God fearing," and doing kind things because they "fear" what is going to happen to their soul if they don't, this defeats the reason why they are being kind in the first place.

Whereas if someone who doesn't believe in the afterlife or in God is kind and loving to others anyway, because they *want* to be kind and loving to others, they are doing this from a purely thoughtful and loving place.

This is the true basis of soul growth.

Are spirits with a person "all" of the time?

Loved ones in spirit are with a person every time they ask them to be, also even at times throughout the day when the spirit either feels their guidance is needed or even when just hanging out with that person. Of course, it depends on the relationship.

Meaning a spouse will usually be with their partner a great deal of time during the day/evening, parents visit on a daily basis, and other relatives drop by every now and then. But this all depends on what is taking place in someone's life.

One of the most-asked questions or thoughts people have and are afraid to ask, because people tend to be embarrassed (but I know is on their mind) is if spirits are with them during, let's just say, their private or intimate times.

And the answer to that is: not to worry, spirits know when to leave a room ...

WHAT IS THE PERSPECTIVE FOR A LOVED ONE IN SPIRIT?

This is what is really amazing and somewhat hard for us here to truly comprehend. As discussed in this book, Heaven is a real place, one that is separated from this world only by physics.

For most here, there is a total separation, but for those in spirit, there is no separation at all, as they experience all that Heaven is along with continuing to experience this world as well. It would be like if there were two large rooms and separating the two rooms was a two-way mirror. Those on one side of the room could not see what was taking place in the other room, whereas those in the other room could see what was taking place in both rooms, as well as being able to be present in either room.

DO LOVED ONES IN SPIRIT GET ANGRY?

The emotion of anger is something that those in spirit usually will not experience, especially toward someone they care about here. Spirits have the foresight of knowing why things have occurred and will occur in life, thereby giving them a greater understanding and perspective.

But spirits can feel disappointment, and this is usually when someone is not living their life to its fullest potential. And when this occurs, that spirit will usually go into overdrive to try to get that person back on track!

WILL MY LOVED ONES IN SPIRIT EVENTUALLY LEAVE ME?

Never!

Just as there is no time limit on love, there is no time limit to your loved ones in spirit being with you. Your loved ones in spirit will always continue to be with you, loving you and guiding you, as you really are a big part of what makes their "Heaven" so great.

WHY ALL THE MYSTERY WITH SPIRITS AND THE AFTERLIFE?

Remember being in grade school and while you were studying, it began to snow? You would run to the window and gaze out with excitement in all the anticipation of the fun and joy that snow was going to bring. Then you heard the sound of the teacher's clapping hands, calling you back to your desk! And as you sat back down in your seat, staring at your book or trying to listen to your teacher, your mind was really still in one place ... the snow!

Although very elementary, this is really sort of the same reason why Heaven and your loved ones in spirit remain unnoticed most of the time. You see, if you knew exactly what Heaven really had in store or could vividly see how often your loved ones in spirit were actually with you, your life would be more focused upon them, and not paying attention to the world around you, thereby not living or learning the lessons needed to be learned.

The same way as if it were to snow …

30. Lighter Side to the Other Side

When I am giving a reading, the messages spirits convey are usually very heartfelt and healing. They come in with love, compassion, and understanding from the spirit to their loved ones who are receiving the readings. When hearing these messages and confirmations, they know, just as I do, that this can bring healing as well as bridge the connection with the ones they love.

But then there are those times when humor comes into play. During a reading, I sometimes will try to slip in my humor, when I find it appropriate, of course. I believe that laughter through tears is the best kind of medicine, and I find that most people feel the same way. Even those in spirit…

MAGIC RICHARD

I once spoke with a woman named Karen who wanted me to make a connection with her wonderful husband in spirit named Richard. During the reading, Richard told her that he had been behaving himself in Heaven but he could not say the same about his Karen.

Hearing this I laughed, asked Richard what he meant by that, and he replied with the word "stripper." I told Karen that Richard was saying something about her in conjunction with a stripper and asked if she had been to see one?

Surprised at what she was being asked, she replied, with determination in her voice, that of course she had not been with a stripper! I told her I knew what I was hearing from her husband and he said stripper. At that, Richard also added he was happy she had a good time!

When I conveyed this to Karen, after thinking for a while, she suddenly burst out laughing! Karen told me that she had recently seen the movie *Magic Mike XXL* (a movie about male strippers with Channing Tatum) with some friends at her house. Karen said while watching it, she became a little embarrassed and had wondered what Richard would have thought about her seeing it. She got her answer.

DON'T LOOK UP

I recently spoke with a man who asked if his wife in spirit was happy that he had been noticing all the various signs he believed she had been giving him. His lovely wife told him she couldn't be happier that he noticed her signs and also how touched she was that he thanked her and gave his love to her with each and every one … especially the "bird ones!"

After she said this to him, they both started to laugh. Not knowing why, I asked, what was so funny about bird signs? The man then explained that he was recently taking a walk outside, thinking about his wife, when suddenly, bird poop dropped on his head!

His wife laughed and responded that although signs can come in many forms, that one was just nature taking its course! She then said if he wanted to connect with her through that particular sign, she would be happy to see what she could do for him in the future …

Spirit in Training

When I connect with a spirit, one of the very first things I will ask those on the Other Side to communicate to me is the manner in which they passed. This information is usually conveyed to me by the spirit giving me some type of sensation or feeling on my body that I can then identify and relate to the type of passing they had experienced.

Recently I made a connection with a young man named Justin who was in spirit. I was speaking with his fiancé Cassie over the phone. I had asked him to communicate his passing to me, and although he had felt no pain with his passing, he did give me the feeling of a sudden impact. Knowing what this usually meant, I asked if he had been in an automobile accident; she replied that he had been struck by a train.

Of course, by any definition, this was a tragic passing, but not to Cassie. Throughout the reading, Justin conveyed to her that he was fine and that he understood the reason he had to pass in such a way, and part of the reason was that it will truly be beneficial to others in ways that cannot be imagined. Cassie understood and took his words to heart.

As the reading was coming to an end, Justin told me that Cassie was going to be taking a trip. Excitedly, she confirmed that she was. He then said to her that he too was going with her, but asked if she would do him a favor.

Cassie replied of course, she would do anything, just name it. And even though I heard his answer, which made me laugh out loud, I hesitated to repeat it. But spirits know that if they tell me something I am going to say it, no matter what.

He said he was up for anything on this vacation, but he told her "just don't take a train ..."

I was happy to hear her laughing as well and she said that was the best confirmation ever as that was just him and his crazy sense of humor!

BETTER LATE THAN NEVER

I was speaking to a young man named Zac who was in his teens, and his older brother Eddie in spirit was discussing the things taking place in his little brother's life. Zac was happy to know that his older brother had been noticing he was doing well in school and also teased him about a girl he had been dating.

In speaking with them, the two seemed to have had a very close relationship, and they still did. During the reading, Eddie wanted me to talk about a watch. Not knowing exactly what he was referring to, I asked Zac if he had his older brother's watch or did he recently buy one. The latter was correct, as he shared that he had just purchased a watch a few weeks before. Okay, I thought. That was just a nice confirmation for the younger brother to know that his older brother was looking after him, even when he was just buying a watch.

But after giving the confirmation, Eddie would not let the subject of the watch go, so I knew there was more. I continued, and asked Zac if he really liked watches? He replied not especially, but just saw it and felt a strong urge to buy it. Okay, now I got it! I knew what Eddie wanted me to say, because when Zac answered this way, his brother was pointing to himself. So, I told Zac that not only did Eddie see him buy the watch, but pushed him into buying that watch.

The younger brother laughed and thought that was pretty cool.

And so, I started to continue the reading when Eddie then again pointed to the watch. *For God's sake*, I thought, *there's even more to this*? So once again, I asked Zac if there was any special reason why he bought the watch, and he could not think of one. Turning back to his brother in spirit, I questioned what the reference was to that watch. With that, he answered "funeral." Okay, I thought, not sure where we're going with this, but I told the younger brother that Eddie was telling me to say funeral.

With that, Zac burst out laughing!

Finally, I said, "I can't wait to hear this one!"

Zac then explained to me that he had to drive in from school to go to his brother's funeral and in his mind, he thought it began an hour later than it did, making him almost miss his brother's funeral!

Eddie also was laughing and said that it was okay, it was better for him to be late than never and he thought the watch might help his brother in the future…

SIGN OF THE TIMES

I once spoke with a woman who was very anxious to hear from her beloved husband in spirit. While speaking with him, he wanted her to know that he knew she would constantly talk to him and that he heard every word. Her husband had a good sense of humor and told his wife that she would even nag him at times. She laughed and said how true that was.

But one of the things she said that she was nagging him about were signs. She told her husband that she kept asking for a sign and had not received any.

He responded that of course she had; in fact, he had given her one over and over again, hoping she would notice. When she asked what the sign had been, he showed me a bed.

With that, I told her what he was showing me and told them both that I may not want to know what this sign meant, making them both laugh. He then explained the bed to me. Her husband conveyed that his wife would often wake up in bed in the middle of the night. When

I told her this, she said that was true! Many nights she would wake up at the exact same time of night, that being 2:40 a.m.

Hearing this and with her husband now smiling, I asked her if 2:40 a.m. meant anything else to her. She thought for a moment and then, in a loud reaction, she yelled out yes!

She said that it was around 2:40 a.m. when the two met for the first time. She had been working a late shift in a casino in Vegas when she bumped, and she meant literally bumped, into her husband, who was wrapping up an evening of gambling. The two started talking, the sparks flew, and they eventually married.

I told both that it was a pretty unusual way for him to give his wife a sign, and next time he might want to just make a light blink. We all laughed.

A week later, this woman wrote to me and said that in the middle of the night, one of her lamps turned on. Okay, maybe I should have asked him to send a sign in the daytime!

SPIRITED CAR KARAOKE

I was once speaking with a woman whose son was in spirit. During her reading, it came up that when she was in the car, she would play her son's favorite songs, as this made her feel his spirit there in the car with her. Although she thought it was just her imagination, it made her happy anyway.

But it was not her imagination. During her session, her son brought up the fact that he was really in the car with her while she would listen to his music. But the love I felt from him for her doing this turned to laughter. I then asked him was he laughing because his mother was a bad singer? He shook his head no, and then he started to eat candy.

Not sure what this meant, I told his mother what her son was doing and she began to laugh and cry at the same time!

She explained that a particular artist her son loved was Eminem. Oh, I thought, that's what the candy was all about, and I told him that was a good one! But he went on to convey that never in his life (or afterlife) did he think he would ever see or hear his mother rapping Eminem songs, or that he would be bobbing his head and rapping right along with her!

So remember, when you're in the car singing by yourself, you never know who's actually listening or singing right along with you ...

LEMON CHESS PIE

Kathy and I were holding a small group event once where a family of four was in attendance. It was a group of siblings—two sisters, two brothers—and they were hoping to hear from their dear mother. I did in fact connect with their mother and she spoke to each one, letting them know what she had been observing, as well as giving them guidance in their life.

But toward the end of the session, their mother started to communicate to me something about a pie. I wasn't sure exactly what she was talking about but I told them that their mother was showing me a pie. They looked puzzled by this, then she showed me the ground. Again, not know exactly what she wanted to covey with this message, I told them she what she was showing me. When I shared this with the group, two of them started laughing, and then reminded the others why.

Every Sunday, all the siblings would go over to their mother's house for a family dinner. It was something she looked forward to as much as they did. Wellon one occasion, the weather was just perfect and their mother decided to set up the table outside, and they all agreed that was a great idea.

So as everyone began finishing their meals, their mother got up from the table and went inside the house. A few moments later, she came out with a surprise she had been working on: a beautiful lemon chess pie!

But as their mother walked from the house to the table in the yard with the pie, something unexpected happened. One of the son's dogs became overly excited and jumped up at the pie, knocking it against her chest. Everyone gasped as she put her arms down, causing the plate to fall to the ground and her body to be covered with lemon filling.

Hearing the recollection of the story made everyone laugh, including Kathy and myself. Of course, I couldn't help but to add my two cents worth and told their mother that it sounded more like she made a lemon "chest" pie. Everyone laughed, even their mother.

Conclusion:
Your Life, My Goal

My goal with the mediumship I do, to put it simply, is one thing: for you to know your loved ones in spirit continue to live, love, and be present with you. I am humbled to do the work I do, but I really never look at it as work, as that implies it is a job.

No, what I do is living.

I feel very fortunate to do what it is that I do, for being a medium. I know that for whatever reason, I was given this gift, which I honor and bring to life with purpose. And that purpose is you. By reading this book, I know that you are at least curious, interested, or even fascinated about life after life and how it connects with your life.

I get it; I continue to find it just as fascinating as at the start of discovering my gift. So, with that, I have dedicated my life to helping those in need gain a better understanding of how connections with loved ones in spirit continue. And such an understanding truly can change one's life … for a lifetime.

———

I remember once giving a reading to someone who thought he had lost it all. His name was Trey. Trey came to me as a last hope, wanting desperately to know if there was any kind of confirmation I could give to him that there really was an afterlife. I could feel his pain, and I hoped I would be able to help him.

Trey had always been good with finances, even made a career of his talent by becoming a financial adviser. He had the cars, he had the houses, and even a beautiful wife Charlotte that he loved dearly.

Trey had to work hard, putting in many hours, not only to get these things, but to keep them. But he felt it was worth it. But what gave Trey the most joy out of life was his beautiful daughter, Brook. To Trey, Brook was everything. A rambunctious six-year-old, she was very much like her father, never taking no for an answer and always doing things her own way.

Trey felt that he and his wife Charlotte were as close as a couple could be, but it was Brook who made his family, and his life, complete. That was until a day came that would change Trey's life forever. During his usual busy day at work, taking calls from investors and such, Trey's personal cell rang, and once he answered, he heard the voice of his wife screaming and crying on the other end.

As he kept telling her to calm down, he tried to understand exactly what she was screaming at him.

It was the news that a parent prays they will never hear, that Brook was dead. At first, Trey sat stunned and in shock. He thought he misunderstood what he had heard, but as Charlotte caught her breath, she repeated the devastating news. Their daughter had just been hit by a car. Hearing this incomprehensible news, Trey dropped his phone and began to sob uncontrollably.

A coworker took Trey home, and once he arrived, he learned the details of what had happened. Brook had wanted to go outside to play in the yard, but Charlotte had told her that they would have to go out later, as Charlotte needed to finish something she had been working on. But being the strong-willed girl she was, Brook was not taking no for an answer and had decided to venture out on her own. For some reason, Brook ran out from the front bushes and onto the road, not giving the oncoming car a chance to stop before striking her.

After Brook's passing and dealing with all of its aftermath, although Trey and Charlotte tried to keep their marriage intact, the grief the two experienced was just too overwhelming and ended up tearing the marriage apart.

Being in such a deep depression after the passing of Brook and his marriage dissolving, Trey had no will to even get out of bed in the morning, much less work. He felt that all the reasons he had dedicated so much of his time to work were no longer there. And all the houses, all the cars, all the stuff just simply vanished in time, leaving Trey living in an old apartment building, one that he used to pass on his way to and from work, never thinking one day he would have lost it all and hide from the world in a small one-bedroom apartment there.

Feeling lost, desperate, and on the verge of ending his life, Trey came to me in hopes of being able to speak with his beautiful daughter once again.

"Your daughter is here and I can tell you, she is full of life. To be honest, she is a little hard for me to connect with as she won't keep still," I said.

Trey nervously replied with tears welling up in his eyes, "That sounds like Brook."

"Well Brook, please try to stand in one place. This will help me to communicate with you," I said to her with a smile.

With that, Brook started to keep still and not move around as much and I continued my connection with her.

"Brook is letting me know first and foremost how much she loves you! She also wants you to know that her passing was not scary at all."

Trey, wiping his eyes as they continued to tear up, replied, "I was so worried that she was afraid or in pain."

With that, Brook showed me a car. "Was this a car accident?" I asked.

"Yes," he quietly replied, "she was struck by a car."

"Well not only was she not afraid, I am also getting that she passed quickly, with no pain at all."

Trey began crying harder. "I was told she had died on the spot."

With that, I felt a loving stubbornness coming from Brook as she conveyed her next message.

"Well Brook strongly wants you to know that she is still with her daddy and her momma."

Trey touched his hand to his heart and said, "She was my heart and soul and daddy loves her so much."

With that, Brook also showed me the figure of a man and a woman being separated.

I asked Trey, "Did you and your wife separate or get a divorce? The reason I am asking this is that Brook is showing me you two apart.

"Yes, we did get divorced. We tried, but it was just too hard to stay together," Trey replied.

"Well Brook wants you to know that it is okay; she knows that you both still love each other very much," I told Trey.

"We do, we really do. But life has been just too hard on the both of us, making it hard to deal with what has taken place," he said.

"She understands this, and is so sorry that you are going through this," I told him.

"It's not her fault, she was just a little girl," Trey said, shaking his head.

"She knows this, but she also says not to blame her momma because it was not her fault either. It really was just an accident," I said.

"I know it was," Trey said, with tears streaming down his face. "Of course, at first, I did blame Charlotte. Why wouldn't I? She was the one who was supposed to watch Brook. I just didn't understand why she didn't keep a better eye on her. But I knew that Brook used to love to hide in the house and Charlotte thought that was all Brook was doing. I'm working on that part."

"Well this makes Brook very happy," I said.

Trey then lifted his head and looked me right in the eye.

"I just wish I could have spent more time with her," he said, with sorrow written all over his face.

I replied, "Brook knows how much you love her and is telling me she loves her daddy very much! She says you don't have to worry that you didn't spend enough time with her because she is able to be with you all the time now!"

"I do feel her with me," Trey replied. "But I know it's just wishful thinking."

Both Brook and I replied strongly to his comment, saying the same thing.

"It's not wishful thinking; it is actually your daughter you are feeling," I replied. "And the more you understand your ability to connect with her, the stronger the connection will be. Brook is also telling me that you can make a lot of things happen, and the one thing she wants you to make happen is to make yourself happy, because she doesn't like to see her daddy with a sad face."

Trey started to smile through his tears when he heard this, and replied, "Gosh, she used to say that to me if she thought I was sad. Sometimes when I was working from home, she would come to me when I was concentrating, thinking I was sad. I used to tell her that I wasn't sad, I just had a lot on my mind. She would then hold her hand to my head and tell me that it was heavy, so I must have a lot on my mind. This would always make us both laugh."

I said with a smile, "That is so cute! Well she is giggling and holding her hand to your head right now, so don't be surprised if every now and then you don't feel a sensation of her touching you there."

After the reading concluded and now understanding that his daughter was truly by his side, Trey had a new lease on life. The experiences he had in the past year helped him to realize that the important things in life are not the things you can buy, but that which is truly the most important: love.

———

Every reading I give means something different to the person receiving it, and I do treat each and every one with the respect they deserve, hoping that the receiver is going to take something away from the experience.

I know I do.

So, whether you already have a strong belief in the afterlife or are someone who is on a journey of discovering their own truths, if there is any (and I mean any) comfort you may receive from my work, I have reached my goal … and you have truly touched my heart.